Michael Price

Windows Vista
for Seniors

in
easy steps

For the Over 50s

In easy steps is an imprint of In Easy Steps Limited
Southfield Road · Southam
Warwickshire CV47 0FB · United Kingdom
www.ineasysteps.com

Notice of Liability
Every effort has been made to ensure that this book contains accurate and current information. However, In Easy Steps Limited and the author shall not be liable for any loss or damage suffered by readers as a result of any information contained herein.

Trademarks
All trademarks are acknowledged as belonging to their respective companies.

Printed and bound in the United Kingdom

ISBN-13 978-1-84078-334-6
ISBN-10 1-84078-334-6

Contents

14 Security & Maintenance   191

15 Help & Support   201

Index   209

1 Get Windows Vista

This chapter will help you choose the best edition of Windows Vista for you. It covers upgrading from a previous version of Windows, or moving up to a more advanced edition of Vista.

Windows Vista

10

Windows Vista is the latest release of Microsoft Windows, the operating system for personal computers. There has been a long list of previous releases including:

- 1995   Windows 95
- 1998   Windows 98
- 2000   Windows Me   (Millennium Edition)
- 2001   Windows XP
- 2003   Windows XP MCE   (Media Center Edition)

When you buy a new computer, it is usually shipped with the latest available release of Windows. This takes advantage of the hardware features generally available at the time. Every year sees new and more powerful features being incorporated into the latest computers. In line with this, the requirements for Microsoft Windows have increased steadily. For example, the minimum and recommended amounts of system memory have increased from Windows 95 (4 MB to 8 MB), Windows 98 (16 MB to 24 MB), Windows XP (64 MB to 128 MB) up to Windows Vista (512 MB to 1024 MB). There's a similar progression in terms of the processor power, the video graphics facilities and hard disk storage.

This means that your computer is likely to need upgrading in order to use a later release of Windows, unless you purchased your computer late in the life of the previous release and it already meets the newer requirements.

The extended hardware options allow the features and services offered by the various releases of Windows to be developed and improved. Each release enhances the existing features and adds new capabilities. Windows Vista is therefore able to provide all of the capabilities of Windows XP and the Media Center Edition operating system, and also offer unique new features.

The value of all this is that you can use your computer to carry out tasks that would not have been possible with previous computers and operating system releases.

Which Release is Installed?

There are several ways to check which release of Windows is installed on your system.

System Properties

1 Press the Windows Logo key and the Break key (simultaneously) to display the System Properties

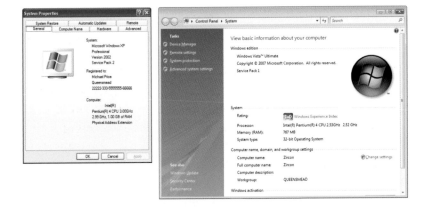

2 The operating system details will be displayed (along with user, memory and processor information)

The Winver Command

1 Press the Windows Logo key and the R key, then type winver and click the OK button

2 The operating system details will be displayed (along with user and memory information)

New Features of Vista

There are hundreds of enhanced features and functions in Windows Vista. Here are some examples.

Visual Style

Windows Vista offers a range of visual styles, so that you can choose the style that you find easiest to work with. The more advanced editions of Windows Vista include a redesigned user interface know as Windows Aero. This includes transparencies, glass effects and window animations and uses a new default font (Segoe UI) with a slightly larger size. Windows Vista also offers Standard (Aero without transparencies and glass effects), Basic (similar to Windows XP but with some aspects of Aero) and Classic (like Windows 2000).

Windows Explorer

Enhancements include a new type of folder known as a Shadow Folder that stores previous versions of modified files, so the folder contents can revert to a point in the past. Graphical thumbnails can be displayed for any file type, not just image files, to show the content. Thumbnails can be zoomed to different sizes. The address bar uses a breadcrumbs view, which shows the entire path to the current location. Clicking any location in the path hierarchy takes you to that level and allows you to re-navigate from there.

Search

Windows Vista integrates search throughout, allowing you to search Folders, Start menu, Help, Control Panel, Networking, etc. The search engine uses indexing to provide instant display of results as you type the search string.

Sidebar and Gadgets

Windows Sidebar is a new panel on the right-hand side of the screen where you can access Desktop Gadgets, small applications (applets) designed for specialized purposes (such as displaying the weather or sports scores). Windows Vista ships with 13 gadgets, and additional gadgets can be downloaded from the Microsoft website.

New and upgraded applications

Windows Mail replaces Outlook Express as the email client.
Windows Contacts, a new contact and personal information
management application, replaces Windows Address Book
(WAB). There's a new Windows Calendar that supports
sharing, subscribing and publishing of calendars. Windows
Fax and Scan allows you to send and receive faxes, and to
send scanned documents as faxes or email attachments.
With Windows Meeting Space, a NetMeeting replacement,
you can share applications or the entire desktop with other
users, on your local network or over the Internet.

Windows Photo Gallery imports from digital cameras and
allows you to tag and rate pictures. It provides basic image
edit, such as color and exposure adjustment, image resize and
crop, red-eye reduction and print. Slideshows, with pan, fade
and other effects, can also be created and burnt to DVD.

Windows Internet Explorer 7

Windows Vista includes the latest version of Internet
Explorer, with tabbed browsing and Quick Tabs, screen
zoom and shrink to fit printing. There are also numerous
security enhancements, including Protected Mode operation.

Security and Safety

This is a major area of improvement, with User Account
Control, Kernel Patch Protection, BitLocker Drive
Encryption and address space layout randomization. In
addition Vista includes a range of parental controls, which
allow you to limit what users of your computer can do.

Networking

Vista has been designed to help you set up and configure
your networks. The "Network and Sharing Center" allows
you to see the status of your network connections, and
to adjust their configurations. Windows Vista also has a
Network Map, which graphically presents how different
devices are connected over the network. Wireless networks
support has also been upgraded.

What's Needed

The minimum configuration needed to install and run Windows Vista on existing hardware is as follows:

- Processor   800 MHz 32-bit or 64-bit
- System memory   512 MB
- Graphics   SVGA (800 x 600)
- Hard disk drive   20 GB (free space 15 GB)
- Optical drive   CD or DVD

Recent computers may have Windows Vista certification, to indicate the version that they can support.

Windows Vista capable PC
This will meet or exceed the above specification, so will run Windows Vista but it may not support Windows Aero.

Windows Vista Premium Ready PC
This will meet a higher specification, including at least:

- Processor   1 GHz 32-bit or 64-bit
- System memory   1 GB
- Graphics   128 MB and WDDM driver
- Hard disk drive   40 GB (free space 15 GB)
- Optical drive   DVD

Express Upgrade to Windows Vista
If you purchased a Windows Vista certified computer, prior to the availability of Windows Vista, you may have received a voucher for an Express Upgrade to Windows Vista. This will allow you to obtain an upgrade copy of Windows Vista free except for a small shipping and handling charge.

The upgrade can be applied to your existing Windows XP system, to install Windows Vista and retain your installed programs, settings and data files. Alternatively, you can choose to apply a full installation, and start afresh.

Hot tip

For resolutions of more than 1280 x 1024, you will need 128 MB graphics memory.

Beware

There may be a cutoff date by which you must redeem the voucher and register for the Windows Vista upgrade.

14

Upgrade Advisor

If you have an older computer, you can have it assessed to see if it is able to support Windows Vista. Visit the website www.microsoft.com/windowsvista/upgradeadvisor and download the Windows Vista Upgrade Advisor.

Run this program to install the Upgrade Advisor and follow the prompts to install and launch the program. This will generate a report to tell you if any changes are needed to support Windows Vista on your computer. It also identifies any incompatible software or accessories that you may have.

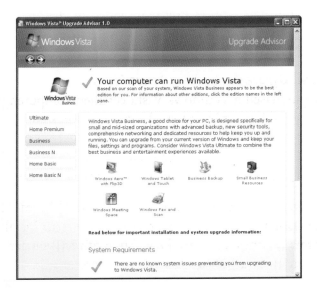

Hot tip

If your computer runs Windows XP, it may already be able to run Windows Vista. Computers running earlier versions of Windows are unlikely to have the necessary capabilities.

Beware

There may be some prerequisite software. You'll be prompted to install this, and you'll then need to restart the Advisor download.

Don't forget

You may find brand specific Windows Vista assessments from computer suppliers. For example, you can download the Vista Readiness Assessment tool from the Dell website.

Vista Editions

Don't forget

These are the main editions, and they are available worldwide. However, you will read about several other editions of Vista, only available in particular regions or to specific groups of users.

You have a choice of four main editions of Windows Vista:

Home Basic
This is for basic home computing, including tasks such as correspondence, email and Internet access.

Home Premium
This provides an enhanced home computing environment and helps you manage collections of documents, pictures, movies, videos, and music.

Business
Groups, organizations and businesses will find this edition more suitable, with its emphasis on organizing, protecting and sharing information.

Ultimate
If you want to combine business and home computing tasks on the same system, this edition gives you the complete combination of features.

There are other editions that are not available to all users. These include:

Enterprise
This is a business edition that is provided to customers such as large corporations that obtain software from Microsoft under the terms of volume license agreements.

European Editions
Europe has two extra editions, Home Basic N and Business N, that exclude the Windows Media Player and related technology.

Don't forget

Starter is the only edition of Windows Vista that will not support 64-bit processors.

Starter Edition
Available only in emerging markets, this edition is low cost but limited in function. It allows up to three simultaneous applications, has restricted graphics capabilities and supports only 384 MB to 1024 MB of memory.

Selecting your Edition

If you are unsure which of these editions of Windows Vista is best for you, it's worth focusing on the features that are excluded from one or other edition.

Features	HB	HP	B	U
Windows Aero visual style	–	Y	Y	Y
Windows Flip 3D	–	Y	Y	Y
Live Taskbar Thumbnails	–	Y	Y	Y
Parental Controls	Y	Y	–	Y
Scheduled backup	–	Y	Y	Y
Windows ShadowCopy	–	–	Y	Y
System image backup and recovery	–	–	Y	Y
Encrypting File System (EFS)	–	–	Y	Y
Windows BitLocker Encryption	–	–	–	Y
Premium games	–	Y	Y	Y
Windows Media Center	–	Y	–	Y
Windows Movie Maker	–	Y	–	Y
Windows DVD Maker	–	Y	–	Y
Tablet PC functionality	–	Y	Y	Y
Touch screen support	–	Y	Y	Y
Windows SideShow	–	Y	Y	Y
Windows Ultimate Extras	–	–	–	Y
Windows Fax and Scan	–	–	Y	Y

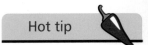

Hot tip

If you choose a lower function edition and discover you do need additional features, you have the opportunity to upgrade your edition to a higher level (see page 18).

If any of these features are ones that you must have, this will limit the number of editions that you need to investigate in detail. In practice, the choice is usually between Home Premium and Business, with Ultimate being the answer if you want both home and business features.

Upgrades

If you are planning to install Windows Vista on an existing computer running Windows XP or Windows 2000, you can purchase an upgrade copy rather than the full copy. The contents are the same, but you pay a reduced price because you are replacing a qualifying operating system.

As an indication of the relative cost of the editions and the saving with an upgrade, the US$ prices at launch time were:

- Home Basic   190.00   99.95
- Home Premium 239.00   159.00
- Business   299.00   199.00
- Ultimate   399.00   259.00

Whichever edition of Vista you choose, the DVD supplied will actually contain all the editions. It is the product key that unlocks your particular edition. This gives you another option – the Windows Anytime Upgrade.

- Home Basic   →   Home Premium
- Home Basic   →   Ultimate
- Home Premium →   Ultimate
- Business   →   Ultimate

① Open the Control Panel and select the System and maintenance option

Control Panel ▸ System and Maintenance ▸   Search

Control Panel Home
• System and Maintenance
Security
Network and Internet
Hardware and Sound
Programs

Windows Anytime Upgrade
Compare features with your current configuration
Upgrade to Windows Vista Home Premium | Upgrade to Windows Vista Ultimate

Administrative Tools
Free up disk space   Defragment your hard drive
Create and format hard disk partitions   View event logs   Schedule tasks

② Locate Windows Anytime Upgrade and click to Compare Features with your Current Configuration

Hot tip

Check at the Microsoft website for your location, or with your software retail store, to find the latest prices for Windows Vista full and upgrade copies.

18

Don't forget

You will also find Windows Anytime Upgrade in the Welcome Center on systems for which this option is available.

3 Review the features offered by your edition of Windows Vista versus the upgrades available

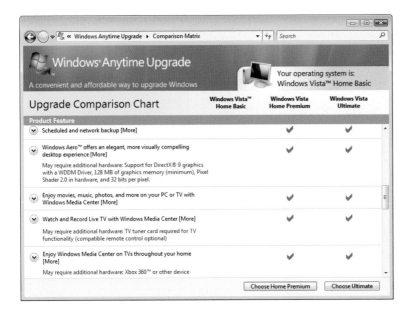

Hot tip

In this example, the current configuration is Home Basic, so this is compared with the Home Premium and the Ultimate editions.

4 Select your preferred option, and you'll be guided through the purchase and the upgrade steps

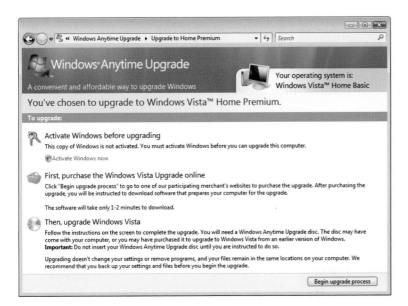

Don't forget

The upgrade will not change your settings and data or remove programs. However, it is still best to ensure that you have a current backup (see page 200).

Activation

Hot tip

Activation is the process by which Microsoft associates your specific copy of Windows Vista with your computer.

Your copy of Windows Vista must be activated before you can apply an upgrade, and in any event within 30 days of first using the system. To check the current status:

1. Select View computer details in the Welcome Center, and click Show More Details

2. Scroll to the bottom of the System details to view the Windows Activation status

Don't forget

If Activation was specified when your system was installed, it will be completed automatically three days after first use.

3. If needed, click Activate Windows Now and follow the prompts to activate your copy of Windows Vista over the Internet

2 The Vista Desktop

The new image of Vista begins with the Welcome Center and the revised Start button. It has a different window structure with a command bar and no menu bar. However, it still supports conventional windows.

Start Windows Vista

Hot tip

The start-up time depends on the configuration of your computer but usually it will be a minute or so.

Switch on your computer to start up the operating system. The stages are as follows:

1 The moving bar with the Microsoft copyright notice shows that the system is being loaded

2 After a few moments the screen clears, then a small Vista logo is displayed and the startup sound plays

3 The Logon screen is displayed, ready for you to enter your password (if defined)

Don't forget

Multiple user accounts will be displayed if your system has more than one defined.

4   The Welcome message is displayed while the user account settings are being applied

Hot tip

If there is only one user account and no password is assigned, Windows skips the Logon screen and goes straight to the Welcome message.

5   The Windows desktop is displayed, with various Windows components, e.g. Taskbar and Sidebar

Don't forget

The specific Windows components displayed will depend on the way in which your system is personalized (see page 36).

23

Desktop Icon   Windows Background   Welcome Center   Windows Sidebar

Sidebar Gadgets

Taskbar

Start Button   Quick Launch Bar   Active Tasks   Notification Area

Welcome Center

This will normally be the first application that appears when you start Windows. It contains just about everything you need to get started with Windows or to resolve any questions or issues that arise with your new operating system. The Welcome Center offers these options:

View computer details   Register Windows online
Transfer files and settings   Windows Media Center
Add new users   Windows Basics
Connect to the Internet   Ease of Access Center
Windows Anytime Upgrade Back Up and Restore Center
What's new in Windows Vista Windows Vista Demos
Personalize Windows   Control Panel

24

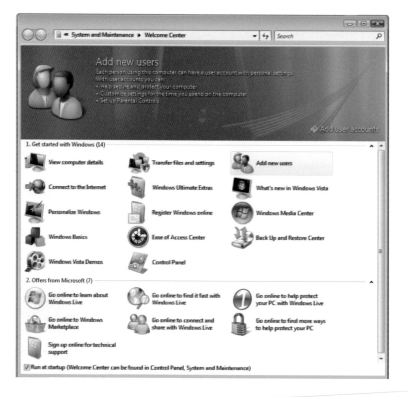

There's also a selection of links from Microsoft, to introduce their Windows Live and Windows Marketplace websites where you can obtain software, services and security tools.

1   Click the Close button [x] to end Welcome Center

Start Button

The usual way to locate Windows applications and functions is from the Start menu. To display the Start menu:

1 Click the Start button on the left of the Taskbar, or press the Windows Logo key on the keyboard

Fixed entries

Recently used entries

Current user

Folders

Settings

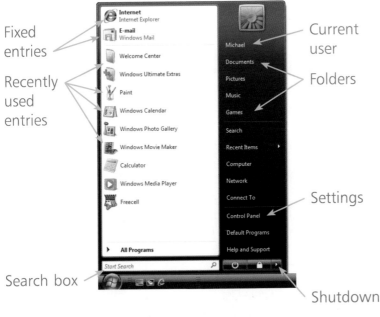

Search box

Shutdown

2 Click an entry to open it

3 Type in the Search box to find a file or programs (see page 95)

4 Click All Programs to list programs and folders of programs and locate the item needed

Don't forget

When you Search, the results are listed on the Start menu in the area used for Fixed and Recently used entries. When you select All Programs or one of its subfolders, the contents are listed in that same area.

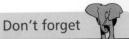

Taskbar

The contents of the Taskbar change dynamically to reflect the activities that are taking place on your computer.

There are a number of components shown on the Taskbar.

Task Buttons

There is a task button for each open window (program or file folder). The selected or foreground task, in this case the Calculator, is shown emphasized. The other tasks are shaded.

Quick Launch Bar

To the left of the task buttons you find the Quick Launch bar. This contains shortcuts to often used tasks, e.g. Show Desktop and Switch Windows.

Notification Area

The portion of the bar on the right is know as the Notification Area and contains icons such as the volume control, the print spooler and Date/Time. These are system functions that are started automatically when Windows starts up.

Language Bar

To the immediate right of the task buttons, you may find the Language bar, which appears when you add text services such as an input language or speech recognition.

Other Toolbars

Right-click an empty part of the Taskbar and select Toolbars to see the other toolbars that can be added.

Don't forget

Inactive icons are hidden, but will be revealed when you click the button to Show All Icons.

...cont'd

By default, the Taskbar is positioned at the bottom of the desktop, but you can move or resize it by dragging. Since this can happen accidentally, the Taskbar is usually locked. To move or resize:

1 Right-click an empty part of the Taskbar and, if there's a check next to Lock the Taskbar, click the entry to remove the check and unlock the Taskbar

> Toolbars ▶
>
> Cascade Windows
> Show Windows Stacked
> Show Windows Side by Side
> Show the Desktop
>
> Task Manager
>
> Lock the Taskbar
> Properties

2 Move the mouse over the edge of the Taskbar until the pointer becomes a double-headed arrow, then drag the border up or down to resize the Taskbar

3 Click an empty part of the Taskbar and hold down the mouse button to drag the Taskbar to one of the four edges of the desktop, then release the button

See page 50 onwards for more details on customizing the Taskbar and the Start Menu.

Click Lock the Taskbar (as described in step 1) to reapply the check and relock the Taskbar, when you've finished moving and resizing.

27

Desktop Icons

Shortcuts to frequently used tasks can also be stored on the desktop. To start with there are standard system icons.

Don't forget

You can change the desktop icons from the default Medium to Large as shown here, or to Classical (small).

1 If no icons are displayed on the desktop, right-click an empty part of the desktop and select View

Hot tip

Some applications add shortcut icons to the desktop when they are installed. You can also create your own shortcuts to any application, file or folder (see page 60).

2 If the entry Show Desktop Icons is not already selected (ticked) then click to select it

3 To specify which system icons to display, right-click the desktop and select Personalize

4 Click Change Desktop Icons and select the icons that you wish to display, or click again to deselect, then click OK to apply the changes

You can click Change Icon to select a new icon image.

Window Structure in Vista

When you open a folder or start a Windows function such as a program, the contents appear on the screen as a window. Vista has introduced some new features to these windows. To view a typical Vista window:

Don't forget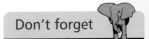

Not all the Windows applications use the new style. See page 31 for an example of a more conventional window.

1   Select Start, and click the Documents folder link

Documents

Features of Vista Windows

Forward and Back buttons

Address bar

Title bar area

Minimize and Maximize buttons

Close button

Search box

Command bar

Headings

Contents pane

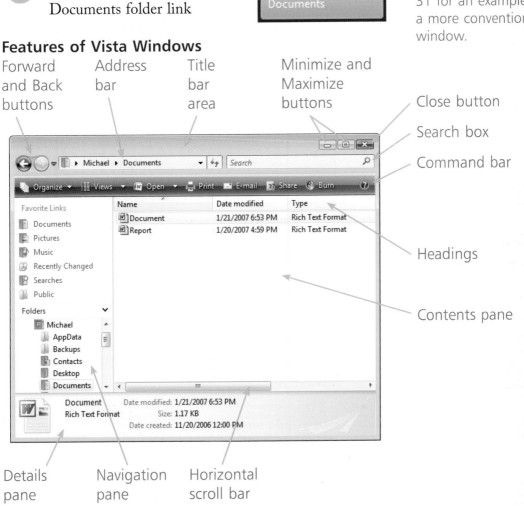

Details pane

Navigation pane

Horizontal scroll bar

2   Click the Maximize button to view the window using the whole screen, and the Restore button will appear in place of Maximize

Move and Resize Windows

Hot tip

Double-clicking the title bar is an alternative to the Maximize button.

Don't forget

You can choose to display the window contents as you drag or, as illustrated here, leave them hidden to improve performance (see page 38).

1 To maximize the window, double-click the title bar area (double-click again to restore the window)

2 To move the window, click the title bar area, hold down the mouse button and drag the window

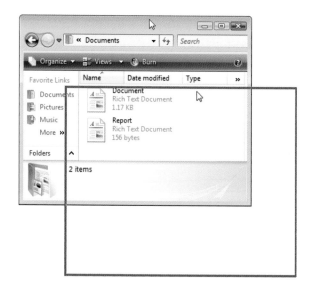

3 To resize the window, move the mouse pointer over any border or any corner, and when the window handle appears, click and drag to the desired size

Application Windows

Application programs, even those included with Windows Vista, still use the traditional window structure, having the Title bar and the Menu bars. For example, the WordPad application window.

 Select Start, All Programs, Accessories and click the WordPad entry, then type some sample text

Don't forget

Some applications may not use all the features. For example the Calculator window has no scroll bars and also cannot be resized.

Features in Application Windows

Control Icon   Title bar   Menu bar   Toolbars

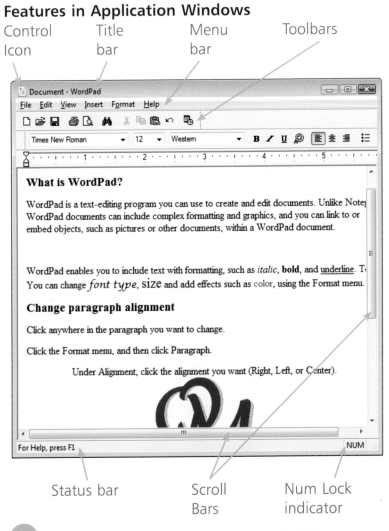

Status bar   Scroll Bars   Num Lock indicator

 You use the same techniques as for the Vista windows, to maximize and restore application windows, and to move and resize them

Menus and Dialogs

The entries on the Command bar and on the Menu bar expand to provide a list of related commands to pick from.

Hot tip

Some entries are toggles that switch on when selected, then switch off when reselected. Note how the associated icons are modified to show the current state, with a frame applied if the option is switched on.

Some entries expand into a submenu, e.g. Organize, Layout.

Other entries open dialog boxes that allow you to apply more complex configurations and settings, e.g. Organize, "Folder and Search Options".

Close Windows Session

When you are ready to end your Windows session, click the Start button and you'll be offered several options.

1 Select the Power Off button to put the computer in Sleep mode, to resume later from where you left off

Within the WordPad document window:

Shutdown Options

Windows Vista offers a power off button (for Sleep or Shutdown), a Lock button and a drop down list of options, including Switch User, Log Off, Lock, Restart, Sleep, Hibernate and Shutdown

NB: This document is in the process of being created and has not been saved

Hot tip

Sleep mode is a low-power state, a combination of Standby and Hibernation. The contents of memory are saved to disk.

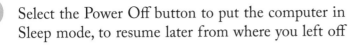

Don't forget

The contents of active applications will be retained, even when you have not saved the data file.

33

Beware

If you normally select Sleep to close your session, you should periodically select the Shut Down option, to refresh the Windows environment.

2 Select the Lock button to display the Switch User screen (thus requiring your password to restore access later)

3 Click the down arrow to select an option from the list provided

Switch User	keep current session and open new
Log Off	end the current session
Lock	password protect the current session
Restart	shut down and restart Windows
Sleep	save session and set low-power mode
Hibernate	save the session and power off
Shut Down	end the session and power off

Change Power Options

Don't forget

You can change the action of the Start menu Power Off button.

Hot tip

Choose Shut Down to close the session and power off the system. The button changes to indicate this action.

Sleep/Hibernate

Shutdown

1 Click Start, type Power Options and press Enter

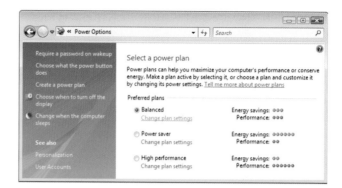

2 Click "Change plan settings" for the active power plan, then click "Change advanced power settings"

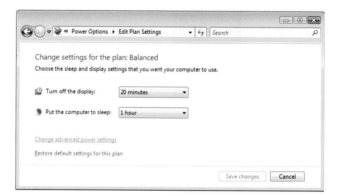

3 Expand the "Power buttons and lid" entry, and then the "Start menu power button" entry, and select your preferred action

4 Click OK to apply the change

3 Personalize Your System

Change the appearance of the Windows Vista desktop. Take advantage of Windows Aero if your system supports this. Select mouse, display and speech options for ease of use.

Personalization Function

The Personalization function allows you to customize many of the features on your system, such as desktop background, screen saver, sounds and monitor settings.

1 Right-click a clear part of the desktop (avoiding the icons and the Sidebar) and click Personalize

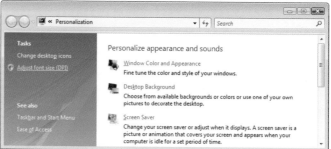

2 For larger fonts, click Adjust font size (DPI) and provide permission to continue, if required

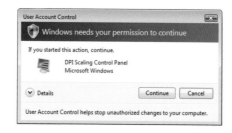

3 Select 120 DPI for a 25% increase in font sizes

...cont'd

4 For other sizes, click Custom DPI and pick 150% or 200% (or drag the ruler)

For a custom DPI setting, select a percentage from the list, or drag the ruler with your mouse.

Scale to this percentage of normal size: 150%
- 100%
- 125%
- 150%
- 200%

9 point Segoe UI at 144 pixels per inch.

☐ Use Windows XP style DPI scaling   OK   Cancel

5 Click OK to apply the selected changes

Hot tip

Dragging the ruler allows you to select any % value between 100% and 500%.

6 You must allow the computer to restart, to see the effects

Microsoft Windows

You must restart your computer to apply these changes

Before restarting, save any open files and close all programs.

Restart Now   Restart Later

7 Reselect the right-click menu on the desktop, and it will now display the text in a larger size

8 Select Personalize, and this dialog box also has larger text

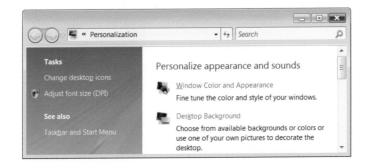

View ▸
Sort By ▸
Refresh

Paste
Paste Shortcut

New ▸

Personalize

37

« Personalization   ▾ | ↔ | Search   🔍

Tasks
Change desktop icons
🔧 Adjust font size (DPI)

See also
Taskbar and Start Menu

Personalize appearance and sounds

Window Color and Appearance
Fine tune the color and style of your windows.

Desktop Background
Choose from available backgrounds or colors or use one of your own pictures to decorate the desktop.

Don't forget

Changing the DPI scaling is usually the better option, since you retain the advantage of larger numbers of pixels, giving a clearer image.

9 Repeat the procedure to reset the font size back to 100% or to try out a different DPI scaling

You can also increase the effective text size by reducing the monitor resolution (see page 45).

Color and Appearance

1 From Personalization, select "Window Color and Appearance"

 Window Color and Appearance

2 The Appearance dialog is displayed, allowing you to choose an alternative color scheme if desired

Hot tip

This shows the options offered for a system that has Windows Vista Basic support enabled.

38

Don't forget

The Effects option also allows you to choose whether or not to show the contents of windows while they are being dragged (see page 30).

3 Click the Effects button to choose the method of edge smoothing for screen fonts

Clear Type font smoothing helps to reduce the jagged appearance of screen fonts by making the edges more detailed. The best effects are achieved with LCD monitors, since display can be controlled to the subpixel level. However, it also offers benefits on CRT monitors, where anti-aliasing is used to achieve the smoothing effect.

Windows Vista includes new fonts that are designed to work with Clear Type. These include Constantia, Cambria, Corbel, Candara, Calibri and Consolas.

...cont'd

The options offered are different for a system that has the Windows Aero support available and enabled.

1. Select "Window Color and Appearance" from the Personalization dialog

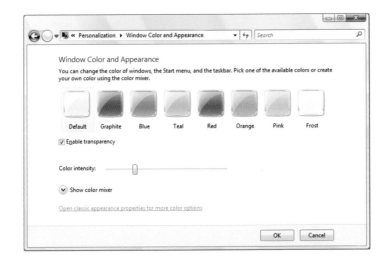

Hot tip

This option does not appear if any color scheme other than Windows Aero is selected.

2. Click "Open classic appearance properties for more color options", to review or change the color scheme and related settings

Don't forget

Appearance Settings has an additional color scheme entry, Windows Aero, when the appropriate graphics hardware and the required edition of Vista are installed.

3. As with Windows Vista Basic, click the Effects button to adjust the font smoothing options

Background

You can choose any of the backgrounds provided or use your own pictures to cover the desktop.

1 Select Desktop Background from the Personalization dialog

2 Click the down arrow to select the picture location, for example Windows Wallpapers

3 Click the up and down arrows ⌃ and ⌄ to collapse and expand the lists of pictures

4 Choose to stretch or replicate the picture to fill the screen, or just center one copy of the image

Screen Saver

You can select a picture or an animation to display while
your computer is idle. This is known as a screen saver.

1 Open Personalization and select the  Screen Saver
Screen Saver option

2 Click the down
arrow to select
a screen saver,
e.g. Photos

3 Click Preview
to see how it
operates

4 Click Settings
to make any
adjustments

Don't forget

There are a number of
screen savers provided
with Windows Vista.

(None)
3D Text
Aurora
Blank
Bubbles
Mystify
Photos
Ribbons
Windows Energy
Windows Logo

Screen Saver Settings

Screen Saver

Screen saver

Photos   Settings...   Preview

Wait: 10   minutes On resume, display logon screen

Power management

Conserve energy or maximize performance by adjusting display
brightness and other power settings.

Change power settings...

OK   Cancel   Apply

Hot tip

Click the box On
resume, display
Logon screen, if you
leave your computer
unattended.

Photos Screen Saver Settings

Use all pictures and videos from Photo Gallery

With this tag:

With this rating or higher:

Any rating

Don't show items tagged:

Use pictures and videos from:

C:\Users\Michael\Pictures   Browse...

This computer's video card can't play themes.

Slide Show speed: Medium

Shuffle contents

How do I customize my screen saver?

Save   Cancel

5 This screen saver will use the contents of your
Picture folder, your Photo Gallery or another folder,
to create a slide show that will run whenever your
computer has been idle for ten minutes

41

Sounds

Windows associates sounds with actions, so you can tell what's happening even if you are not looking at the screen. There's a set of default sounds, or you can add your own.

Hot tip

Choose No Sounds from the list of Sound Schemes if you do not want audio prompts.

Don't forget

Clear the box labeled "Play Windows Startup sound", to suppress the sound when you start up the system.

1 Select the Sound option from the Personalization dialog   🎵 Sou<u>n</u>ds

> **Sound**
>
> Playback | Recording | **Sounds**
>
> A sound theme is a set of sounds applied to events in Windows and programs. You can select an existing scheme or save one you have modified.
>
> Sound S<u>c</u>heme:
>
> [Windows Default ▾] [Sa<u>v</u>e As...] [<u>D</u>elete]
>
> To change sounds, click a program event in the following list and then select a sound to apply. You can save the changes as a new sound scheme.
>
> Program
>
>   Menu pop-up
>   Minimize
>   New Fax Notification
>   New Mail Notification
>   Open program
>   Print Complete
>
> ☑ <u>P</u>lay Windows Startup sound
>
> Sounds:
>
> [Windows Notify.wav ▾] [▶ <u>T</u>est] [<u>B</u>rowse...]
>
> [OK] [Cancel] [Apply]

2 To hear the sound that belongs to an action, select the task name and click the Test button

3 Click the down-arrow next to Sounds to choose another .wav file, or click Browse to search the disk for a suitable audio file

Sounds:

[Windows Notify.wav ▾]

(None)
ac3
chimes.wav
chord.wav
ding.wav
dts
ir_begin.wav
ir_end.wav
ir_inter.wav
notify.wav
recycle.wav
ringout.wav
Speech Disambiguation.wav
Speech Misrecognition.wav
Speech Off.wav
Speech On.wav
Speech Sleep.wav
tada.wav
Windows Balloon.wav
Windows Battery Critical.wav
Windows Battery Low.wav

4 When you've modified the sound scheme, Click Save As to keep a copy

> **Save Scheme As**
>
> <u>S</u>ave this sound scheme as:
>
> [My Sound Scheme]
>
> [OK] [Cancel]

Mouse Settings

Changing the settings for your mouse might make it much easier to work with Windows.

1 Select Mouse Pointers from the Personalization dialog

 Mouse Pointers

2 If you have difficulty spotting the mouse on the display, try an alternative scheme such as Extra Large

3 Click the Pointer Options tab, and you can apply a number of useful changes to help with using the mouse:

- Change the speed at which the pointer moves

- Automatically place the mouse pointer over the default button, when you switch windows

- Display a trail as you move the pointer, so it is easy to see

- Show the location of the pointer when you press the Ctrl key

...cont'd

Using the mouse can sometimes be a problem for left-handed users. If this applies to you, Windows provides a possible solution.

1 Click the Buttons tab in Mouse Properties

2 Choose "Switch primary and secondary buttons"

3 Double-click the folder and if it does not open or close consistently, try a slower setting

4 ClickLock lets you highlight or drag without holding down the mouse button – all that's needed is a brief click to set or remove the click lock

Monitor Resolution

 From the Personalization dialog, select Display Settings

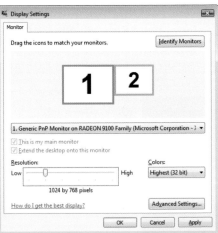

Beware

The resolutions and color settings offered depend on the type of monitor and the type of graphics adapter that you have on your computer.

2 Drag the slider to select the resolution you prefer

3 You can change the color depth by clicking the down-arrow (the highest level is usually the best choice)

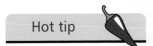

Hot tip

The higher the resolution the more you can fit onto the screen, but the smaller the text and images will appear (unless you choose a higher DPI scaling, see page 36).

4 Click Advanced and the Monitor tab to set the Refresh rate

Don't forget

Make sure that the "Hide modes that this monitor cannot display" box is selected, so that only usable refresh rates are displayed. Again, higher rates give more comfortable viewing.

5 Click the Apply button to make the changes

Accessibility Options

 Select the "Ease of Access" link in the Personalization dialog

See also
Taskbar and Start Menu
Ease of Access

 Alternatively, click Start, Control Panel, "Ease of Access" then click "Ease of Access Center"

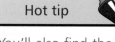

Hot tip

You'll also find the "Ease of Access Center" by clicking Start, All Programs and then "Ease of Access".

46

3 The "Ease of Access Center" opens with a narrator reading the introductory text and listing the main accessibility tools offered

4 Clear the boxes to turn off the narrative on future visits to the Accessibility Center, if preferred

 Press the spacebar to start one of the tools, for example Magnifier, to see how it might help you

Magnifier

This enlarges a portion of the display in a separate window. It follows the mouse pointer or the keyboard focus (tab and arrow keys) or text input whichever is currently active.

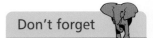

Don't forget

The magnifier is not just for text, it is also very useful for close-up views of images of all types, including graphics, buttons and pictures.

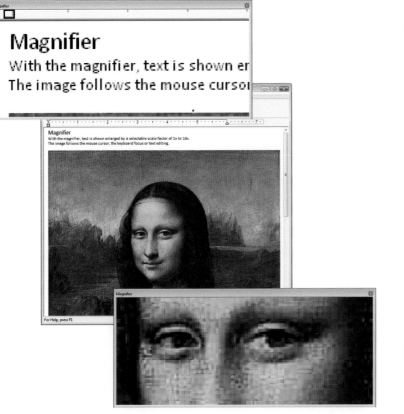

47

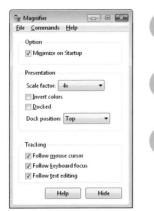

1. Clear "Minimize on Startup" to display the dialog initially

2. To change the zoom level, pick a new scale factor (1x – 16x)

3. Change the tracking options to control which areas of the desktop Magnifier will enlarge

Hot tip

If the Magnifier dialog is not displayed on the screen, right-click the Taskbar button and select Restore.

...cont'd

The "Ease of Access Center" also includes groups of settings to suit various scenarios. Select the ones that may apply to your situation, and it will offer suitable adjustments which will be automatically applied, every time you start Windows.

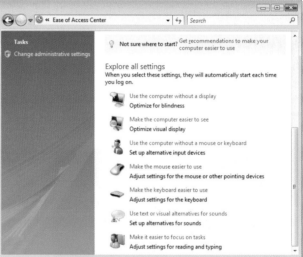

If you are unsure which options to select, select the link "Get recommendations to make your computer easier to use". This displays a five-part questionnaire.

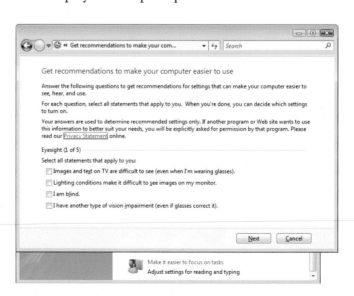

4 Taskbar and Start Menu

Folder and application windows are switched and managed with the Taskbar and Start Menu. Windows Aero adds Flip 3D and live thumbnails.

Taskbar Properties

To make changes to the Taskbar settings:

See also
Taskbar and Start Menu
Ease of Access

1 Select the "Taskbar and Start Menu" link in the Personalization dialog

2 Alternatively, right-click an empty part of the Taskbar and select Properties from the menu

Hot tip

The Taskbar and its contents and methods of resizing and moving it are described on page 26.

Don't forget

Some properties are only available when the Windows Aero scheme is active, for example "Show window previews".

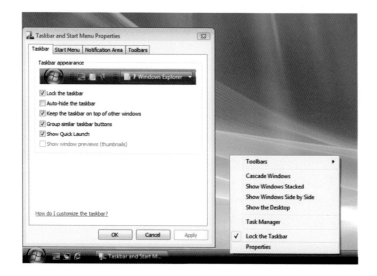

50

3 You can lock and unlock the Taskbar from the Properties dialog as well as from the right-click menu

4 Click the box labelled Auto-hide the Taskbar, to make the full depth of the screen available

5 It reappears when you move the mouse to the usual Taskbar location (e.g. the bottom edge of the screen)

Beware

If you have relocated the Taskbar (see page 26) you'll need to move the pointer to that new location.

Quick Launch Bar

① Clear or select the box labeled Show Quick Launch

Notification Area

① Select the tab Notification Area, and clear or select the box Hide Inactive Icons

② Choose the system icons that should always be displayed

③ Press the Customize button to control how the icons should behave

④ Select an icon (current or past item), click the down-arrow and choose the required behavior

Toolbars

① Select the Toolbars tab to specify which toolbars should appear on the Taskbar

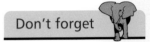

Don't forget

Power is selectable for Laptop PCs only, while Network requires some form of network connection.

51

Don't forget

This provides an alternative to the menu method of selecting toolbars (see page 26).

Taskbar Buttons

Each time you open a window, a taskbar button is added.

1 Click Start and select entries from the main Start Menu, e.g. Computer and then Welcome Center

2 Click Start, and open an application, e.g. Calculator and then WordPad

As you open new windows, the names of the taskbar buttons are truncated, to fit them all onto the taskbar. Move the mouse over a button, and the tool tip shows the full name.

3 When you add more windows, similar windows will be grouped together on the same taskbar button

4 Click a button that has a down-arrow (i.e. multiple tasks) to display the names

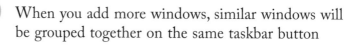

You can see from this that Computer and Welcome Center are both managed by the Windows Explorer application.

...cont'd

With Windows Aero active, there will be some differences, in appearance and in the options available.

1 Click Start and open windows, e.g. Computer, Welcome Center, Calculator and WordPad

When you move the mouse over a button, a thumbnail of the actual window contents is shown, as well as the tool tip.

2 When you add more windows, similar windows are again grouped together

3 Click the down-arrow to display all the names, and move over a name to see its thumbnail image

Hot tip

Windows transparency effects and windows thumbnails illustrated here require Windows Aero to be enabled.

Don't forget

You can disable the windows thumbnails by deselecting "Show window previews" in the Taskbar properties (see page 50).

Switching Tasks

When you have a number of windows open, you'll want to be able to switch between tasks. There are numerous ways in which Windows helps you do this efficiently.

1 Click any part of an open window to switch to it and bring it into the foreground

Don't forget

Windows may overlay one another on the screen, so it may be difficult to find the one you want.

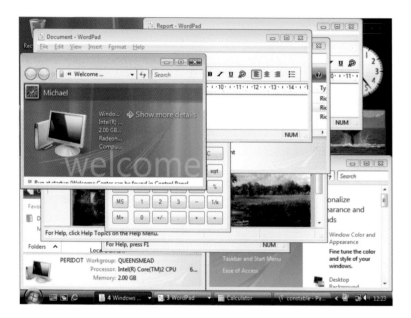

2 Click the Taskbar button for the window you want, to open it (if minimized) and make it the active task

If there are several tasks on the button, click the button and select the window from the name list

Hot tip

Press Alt+Tab, the press the arrow keys to scroll forward or backward through the list of window icons.

3 Hold down Alt, then press Tab several times and release Alt when the required task appears

4 Click Switch Between Windows on the Quick Launch bar, press the arrow keys or Tab to find the task, then press Enter

This provides the same display as Alt+Tab, but it remains on screen until you press Enter or click an icon window

Don't forget

The Cascade Windows and Show Windows options will not show windows minimized to the Taskbar, except when they are applied to a particular Taskbar button.

5 Right-click an empty part of the Taskbar and select Cascade Windows, and click the window you want

55

6 Right-click a button with multiple tasks, and select Cascade, and it will cascade all the windows in the group (including minimized windows)

Hot tip

Select Show Desktop to minimize all the windows, then cascade the group that you want to work with.

Switching with Aero

Hot tip

This illustrates the characteristic transparency feature of Windows Aero.

When the Windows Aero color scheme is supported and active, the Vista Basic window selection techniques continue to work despite the differences in appearance.

1 Click an open window to bring it to the foreground

Don't forget

The associated thumbnail appears when you hover the mouse pointer over the task button or the name on the task list.

2 Click the Taskbar button to select a window, now using the thumbnails to help to identify the specific window required

3 You get the list of names when you select a button with multiple tasks, and you can view the associated thumbnail for any of the tasks

4 With Aero, Alt+Tab shows the thumbnails rather than the icons for the windows (and the desktop)

Hot tip

Press Alt+Tab once to switch to the previous window (this applies to Vista Basic and to Windows Aero).

5 The Quick Launch bar Switch Between Windows provides a new format known as Flip 3D, with large, angled views of all the windows filling the screen

Hot tip

Press Tab or arrow keys to cycle through the windows, somewhat like shuffling a pack of cards.

Don't forget

You must hold down the Windows Logo key to keep the Flip 3D view on the screen. Again you can press Tab or Arrow keys to select a window.

6 The key combination Windows Logo + Tab (active in Windows Aero only) also shows the Flip 3D view

7 The Cascade and Show options for windows and for task groups are the same in Windows Aero as those provided in Windows Vista Basic

Start Menu Properties

The "Taskbar and Start Menu" properties also control how the Start menu appears and which entries will be displayed.

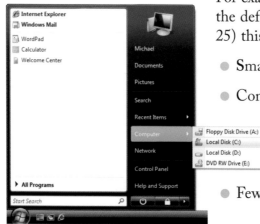

For example, compared with the default style (see page 25) this Start menu has:

- Small icons
- Computer as a menu
- Fewer entries on the list

Don't forget

Choose Classic Start Menu if you prefer the style used by previous releases of Windows.

To make changes to the Start menu:

1 Right-click the Start button and select Properties (or click the Start Menu tab on "Taskbar and Start Menu Properties")

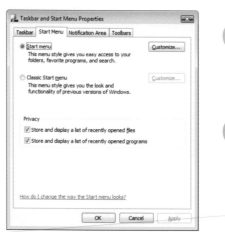

2 Pick "Start menu" to get the Windows Vista style menu

3 Clear the boxes in the Privacy section to stop keeping records of recently opened files and programs

Hot tip

Clear the boxes and click Apply, then reselect the boxes, to start afresh with the lists of recently used files and programs.

4 Click the Customize button to make changes to the Start menu actions and appearance

⦿ Start menu [Customize...]

1 Choose Display as Menu to show a list for an entry such as Computer

2 Clear the box to hide entries such as Default Programs

3 Scroll down to review all the entries and options provided

Don't forget

Exit Customize Start Menu and click Apply, to activate changes.

Other options offered include drag-and-drop menu entries, highlight newly installed programs, open submenus by pausing over them, and set search parameters, as well as more display/no display items. For example, you can:

1 Choose to sort the All Programs menu alphabetically

2 Display the system administration tools

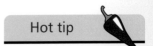

Hot tip

Click the Use Default Settings button to discard all the changes that you have made.

Use Default Settings

3 Use small or large icons for programs on the first level of the Start menu

4 Specify how many recently used programs to display on the Start menu (default is 9)

5 Show or hide the fixed entries for Internet and email at the top of the Start menu

Create Shortcuts

You can create shortcuts to programs or files and place them on the desktop or put them in a folder.

Hot tip

You can create shortcuts to any type of file including documents, drives, folders, network devices and printers.

1 Right-click an empty part of the desktop or folder and select New, Shortcut

2 The shortcut wizard starts up and prompts for the item

Don't forget

If you know the file location, type it and press Next immediately.

3 Click Browse and navigate the folder structure to find the file icon and click OK

4 Click Next to accept the selected file location

5 Accept the suggested name (or type a new name) and click Finish to create the shortcut

There's a quick way to create a shortcut on the desktop.

1 Locate the file, right-click the file icon and select Send To, Desktop (create icon)

2 Create Shortcut will put the shortcut in the same folder

3 Click "Pin to Start Menu" to put the shortcut on the Start menu (applies to program icons and shortcuts only)

Hot tip

Use Search (see page 80) to locate the file for which you'd like to create a shortcut.

61

Beware

Installing Word Viewer may change the icon for .rtf files and shortcuts (see page 127).

Don't forget

Drag a shortcut of any type onto the Start button, then when the Start menu opens, drag and drop the shortcut onto the menu.

Classic Start Menu

If you switch to the Classic Start Menu (see page 58) you'll find it uses the fold-out style from Windows 2000 and Me.

The Customize dialog for the Classic Start Menu offers similar options to the Windows Vista version. However there are some features, such as recently used programs and menu display format, that are not supported in Classic mode.

1 To return to Vista style, open "Taskbar and Start Menu Properties", click the "Start menu" option and then click Apply

5 Gadgets and Devices

Windows Sidebar provides small applications or gadgets that offer useful functions and information. Hardware devices such as USB flash drives can be used to boost performance. Use SideShow to view email without turning on your computer, if it has an auxiliary display.

Windows Sidebar

Windows Sidebar provides another way to run tasks, with its Gadgets, which are small, easy-to-use and customizable mini-applications.

There's a collection of gadgets included in Windows. Three of these appear on Sidebar in the default configuration: Clock, Slide Show and Feed Headlines. To see the others:

Don't forget

Gadgets offer information at a glance. They can connect to web services, for example weather, news or traffic updates.

1. Click the Add symbol at the top of Windows Sidebar to display the first page of Gadget Gallery

Don't forget

There may be a different selection of gadgets on your system.

2. Click the arrow to see the next page of the gallery

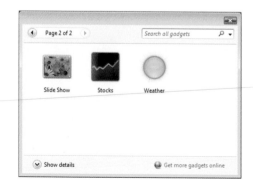

Add and Remove Gadgets

Point to any one of the gadgets and two buttons appear on the right and near the top. These are Close and Options.

1 Click the Close button to remove that gadget from the Sidebar (it will stay in the local Gadget Gallery)

2 Click the Options button to display its particular options

With the Slide Show gadget, the Options allow you to choose where to search for pictures, how long to display each picture, the transition effect between slides (if any) and whether you want random sequence (Shuffle).

For the Clock gadget, you can choose the appearance, assign a name, specify the time zone and show the second hand. You can also reset the computer time.

3 Open the Gadget Gallery and double-click a gadget to add it to the Sidebar

4 When you've finished with the Sidebar, right-click the Sidebar icon in the Notification area and select Exit, to release the deskspace for the rest of the session

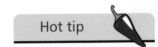

Hot tip

Add another copy of the Clock gadget and set them to different time zones.

65

Don't forget

Windows Sidebar will display the next time you start Windows unless you change the settings (see page 66).

Sidebar Properties

To view and change the Windows Sidebar properties:

 1 Right-click Windows Sidebar and select Properties

2 Clear the box Start Sidebar when Windows starts, to prevent it starting automatically

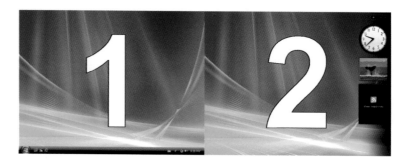

Windows Sidebar Properties

Sidebar

☑ Start Sidebar when Windows starts

Arrangement

☐ Sidebar is always on top of other windows

Display Sidebar on this side of screen:
◉ Right
○ Left

Display Sidebar on monitor: 1 ▾

Maintenance

View list of running gadgets

Restore gadgets installed with Windows

How do I customize Windows Sidebar?

OK   Cancel   Apply

3 Choose Sidebar is always on top, to have it visible at all times

4 Position Sidebar on the right or on the left of the screen

5 If you have dual monitors on your computer, you can choose to put Sidebar on either display

Restart Sidebar

If you Exit Sidebar, or choose not to start it with Windows, you can run it from the Start Menu.

1 Click the Start button, type Sidebar in the Search box, and click Windows Sidebar from the results list

Programs
Windows Sidebar
Windows Sidebar Properties
See all results
Search the Internet

sidebar

Get More Gadgets

Windows Vista provides a basic set of gadgets, but you can download more gadgets from the online Gadget Gallery.

1 Right-click Windows Sidebar and select Add Gadgets… to open the local Gadget Gallery

Bring Gadgets to Front
Add Gadgets…

Properties
Help

Close Sidebar

2 Click the link "Get more gadgets online"

🌐 Get more gadgets online

3 View "Top downloads" or "Top rated", or "See all gadgets"

4 Choose a gadget, for example Calculator and click Download

5 Download and install the gadget onto Windows Sidebar

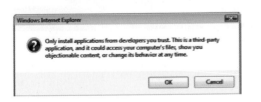

Windows Internet Explorer

❓ Only install applications from developers you trust. This is a third-party application, and it could access your computer's files, show you objectionable content, or change its behavior at any time.

OK   Cancel

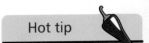

Hot tip

There is a growing number of gadgets provided by third parties and made available through the Microsoft Vista Gallery.

67

Don't forget

Follow the prompts to download and install the gadget. There's no need to save the file to your hard disk, it can be installed directly to the Sidebar.

Place Gadget on Desktop

You can detach a gadget from the Sidebar and place it on the desktop. To transfer a gadget:

1 Move the mouse over the gadget then click and hold the mouse button

2 Drag the gadget over the line at the edge, until it is completely off the Sidebar

3 Position the gadget somewhere on the desktop then release the mouse button

4 You can right-click the Sidebar and select Close, to hide the Sidebar, leaving the re-positioned gadgets on the desktop

5 Right-click and select Open to redisplay the Sidebar

Install New Device

Most devices can be installed by plugging them into your computer. Windows will add the required driver software if it is available (or prompt you for the CD that came with the hardware).

To install a USB device such as a flash drive:

1 Insert the device into one of your USB port

2 Windows identifies the device (1 GB Verbatim drive) and begins installing the driver software required

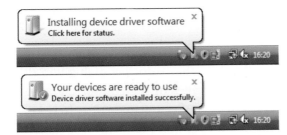

3 Installation completes and the device is ready to use

4 The AutoPlay dialog will offer you options to view or work with the contents

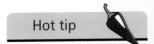

Hot tip

Hardware devices are usually attached to a USB (Universal Serial Bus) port on your computer.

Beware

Your particular device may require you to install the software before plugging in the hardware. Always check the instructions before you start the installation.

Don't forget

The options offered on the AutoPlay dialog will differ, depending on the file types of the contents, and the device characteristics (see page 70).

Safely Remove Hardware

Beware

Removing the device without checking that data transfer has completed could be fatal for both data content and device.

When you've finished working with the USB storage device, you should make sure that the computer has finished saving any information before you unplug the device.

1 Wait until the activity light stops flashing

2 If there's a Safely Remove Hardware icon in the notification area, click this and select the device

> Safely remove USB Mass Storage Device - Drive(G:)   ✓ ⓞ ⧉ ⬚ ⁴ˣ 16:47

3 Remove the device when you are told it is safe to do so

> **Safe To Remove Hardware**
>
> This device can now be safely removed from the computer.
>
> OK

The options offered on the AutoPlay dialog will differ, depending on the file types of the contents, and the device characteristics. For example, a generic 256 MB USB 2.0 drive with various files stored generates this panel.

Don't forget

The exact details listed on the dialog will depend on the type of files that Windows detects.

When there is more than one removable drive, the Safely Remove Hardware icon gives a list of available drives.

ReadyBoost

Windows can use the storage space on some removable devices such as USB drives to speed up your computer. The AutoPlay dialog offers this as an option when you insert the device.

1 Choose the option "Speed up my system"

2 Select "Use this device"

3 Specify how much of the storage to reserve for the system

4 To stop using the space, open the device properties and choose "Do not use this device"

71

Not all USB storage devices are capable of being used for this purpose. For example, the generic drive is tested the first time it is inserted, and the results show that it is unsuitable.

Testing is switched off and the ReadyBoost option will not be offered the next time this drive is inserted.

Windows SideShow

Windows SideShow is a new feature in Windows Vista that supports an auxiliary display. These are being specified for notebook and desktop computers and in other devices.

On the auxiliary display, you can work with information such as emails, calendar data, media player status and weather updates, without having to run the main computer.

To see SideShow in action, you need to have a SideShow-compatible device running. These aren't yet widely available. However, Microsoft has a SideShow simulator that mimics a SideShow device, so you can see how SideShow works, even if you don't yet have the hardware.

1 Attach your SideShow device application (or start the VirtualSideShow simulator)

The SideShow simulator comes with three gadgets – the Welcome overview and the games Reversi and Columns.

...cont'd

To specify additional gadgets:

1 Select SideShow from Hardware and Sounds in the Control Panel

Hardware and Sound
Play CDs or other media automatically
Printer
Mouse
Windows SideShow

2 Specify new gadgets, for example Inbox – Windows Mail and Windows Media Player

3 Use the arrow keys and the OK key to select a gadget and scroll its functions

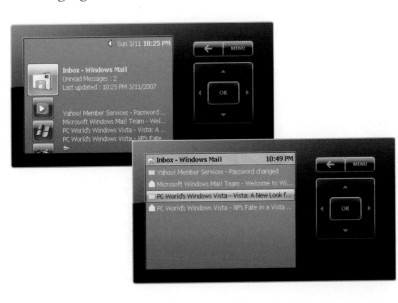

Hot tip

You can download more gadgets from the Internet. There's even help available to create your own gadgets.

Install Printers

When you directly connect a printer to your computer, Windows will normally detect it and add the driver, e.g.:

1 Connect a USB printer such as the Xerox M750

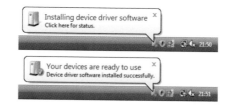

2 Windows detects the printer and installs the driver

3 The printer will be added to the printers folder

Printer not Recognized

1 If Windows does not recognize a printer (e.g. the Samsung CLP-500) it will ask for the driver location

2 Select the option "Locate and install driver software", to continue with the printer installation

> **Found New Hardware**
>
> Windows needs to install driver software for your SamsungCLP-500
>
> ● Locate and install driver software (recommended)
> Windows will guide you through the process of installing driver software for your device.
>
> → Ask me again later
> Windows will ask again the next time you plug in your device or log on.
>
> ● Don't show this message again for this device
> Your device will not function until you install driver software.
>
> Cancel

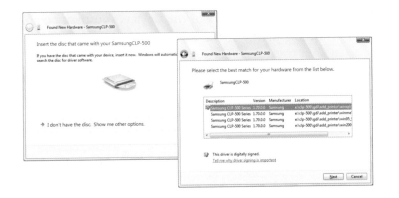

Don't forget

You can try the driver that is designed for Windows XP, if there's no Windows Vista driver available.

3 Insert the disk provided with the printer and select the most appropriate driver from the list

4 Windows installs the driver software (along with the usual Notification area messages)

5 The new printer is added to the Printers folder, but not as the default printer, if there's another printer already installed.

Drivers on the Web

If Windows does not recognize the device, you may be able to find a suitable driver at the manufacturer's website.

As an illustration, on the test system the installed Creative Soundblaster X-Fi audio card wasn't recognized, and so appeared as an unknown Multimedia Audio Controller in Device Manager.

To obtain a Windows Vista driver:

 Visit the www.creative.com/support/vista website and select your region

2 Click the link for the Vista driver availability chart

3 Select the driver link for your particular device

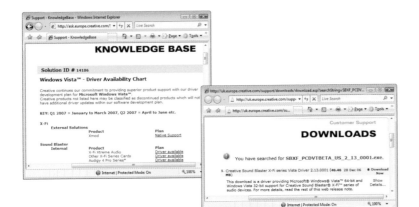

4 Select Download Now, agree license terms as requested then Save the file

5 Specify the location on your hard disk to store the file

6 Double-click the file icon for the downloaded program to begin the installation

---

Don't forget

Each manufacturer's website will have a different setup, but you should look for the support area and search for information on Vista drivers.

77

...cont'd

7 Run the installation program, making sure that other applications have been closed

8 The Windows drivers for the device will be updated

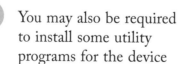

9 You may also be required to install some utility programs for the device

When the installations are completed, you may be asked to restart the system, and you will see the new details in Device Manager.

Control Panel

The Control Panel allows you to change settings for the hardware and software components in Windows.

 Click the Start button and select Control Panel

Don't forget

The exact contents of the Control Panel will depend on the particular configuration of your computer.

 Click any category to explore Control Panel contents

Beware

The same entry may appear in more than one category. For example, Windows SideShow (see page 72) will be added to "Hardware and Sound" as well as Programs.

You can switch to another category from the list on the left.

Regional Settings

The Control Panel allows you to make changes to the regional settings on your computer.

1 Select the "Clock, Language and Region" category

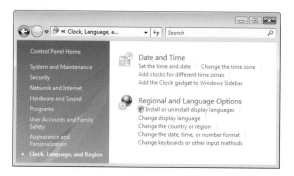

Don't forget

You can define additional taskbar clocks to show the time in other zones.

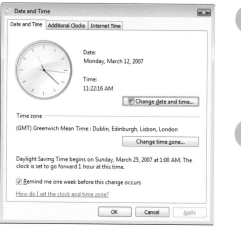

2 Select "Date and Time" to make adjustments or to change the time zone

3 Click the Internet Time tab to reset the time from an online clock

4 Select "Regional and Language Options" to set the display language, select the location (country or region) and choose the keyboard type

80

6 Search and Organize

Windows Vista helps organize the files and folders on your hard disk. Data is stored by username with separate folders for different types of files, or you can add new folders. Powerful instant search facilities help you find your way around all of the folders and the menus.

Files and Folders

The hardware components are the building blocks for your computer but it is the information on your disk drive that really makes your computer operate. There is a huge number of files and folders stored there. To get an idea of how many:

1 Click the Start button and select Computer then select the system disk, e.g. the C: drive

2 Double-click the drive to open it

3 Press Ctrl+A to select all the items

4 Right-click the selection and click Properties

5 This example (Vista Ultimate but no other applications) shows over 40,000 files and 7,000 folders

6 There's even more stored on the disk, as you'll find if you reveal hidden and system files (see page 98)

With so many files and folders to deal with, they must be well organized to ensure that you can locate the documents, pictures and other data that you require. Windows helps by organizing the files into related sections:

- Program Files   Application programs
- Windows   Operating system programs and data
- Users   Documents, pictures, etc.

These are the top-level folders on your hard disk, and each of them is divided into subfolders. For example, the Program Files folder is arranged by supplier and application.

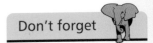

Don't forget

The Program Files and Windows folders are managed by the system, and you will not normally need to access them directly.

1 Open the C: drive and click the Folders bar to show the structure

Folders ⌃

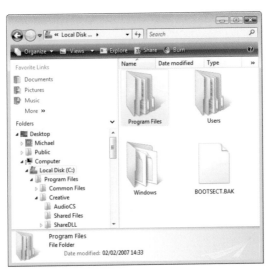

Hot tip

The Users folder contains Document, Pictures, Music and other folders listed on the Start menu (see page 25).

2 Click the white triangles to expand drive, folder and subfolder contents

3 Select the Windows folder and expand the subfolders to see a similar arrangement by system application and function

83

New User Account

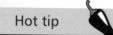
1 Select Start, Control Panel and in User Accounts and Family Safety click "Add or remove user accounts"

User Accounts and Family Safety
Set up parental controls for any user
Add or remove user accounts

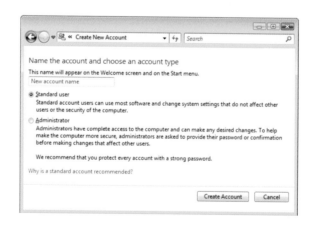

2 Click the option to "Create a new account"

3 Specify the account name and choose the account type

Susan

◉ Standard user

It is recommended to create a standard user account for every user to minimize the risk of unintended changes.

4 Click the Create Account button

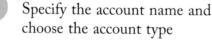

Create Account

The Manage Accounts dialog will be displayed. You can now add a password to the account.

1 Select the account that you want to change

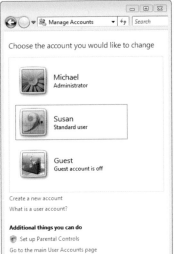

2 Select the change, e.g. "Create a password"

3 Type a password, then re-enter it to confirm

You are recommended to use a strong password. This should be at least eight characters, with mixed upper case, lower case, numbers and symbols, avoiding words and names.

4 Type a password hint if desired then click Create Password

85

User Folders

1 Open the C: drive, display the Folders bar and expand the list for the Users folder

2 There's a subfolder for each user account name defined, plus the Public subfolder

3 Expand the active user account, in this case Michael

4 Select another user account folder, for example Susan

Each user folder (including Public) has a similar set of subfolders defined.

Further up the list, you'll see a second entry for the active user, under the Desktop.

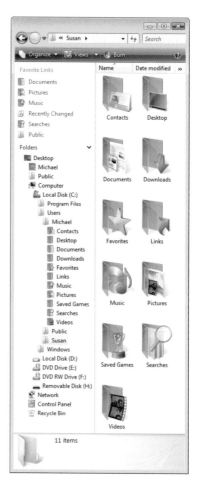

In addition, the Desktop contains entries for Public, Network, Control Panel and Recycle Bin. These entries are just pointers, not actual folders and are designed to provide quick links to the most required parts of the system.

There are also links to Public and some of the active user's folders in the Favorite Links.

Folder Navigation

When you open a drive or folder, you'll find a number of different ways to navigate among the folders on your disk.

1 Open the Documents folder on the Start menu

Address bar   Contents pane   Search box

Forward and Back buttons

Navigation pane

Favorite links

Folder bar

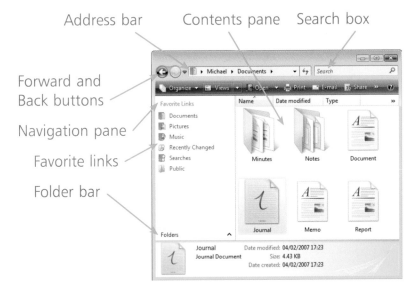

2 To go directly to a location on the Address bar, just click that location

3 To go to a subfolder of a location on the Address bar, click the arrow at the right, and select a subfolder from the list

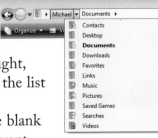

4 To type a location, click the blank space to the right of the current location, to display the current folder path

Type the full path for the new location, for example C:\Users\Public\Documents, and then press Enter

Hot tip

Click the Forward and Back buttons to navigate through locations you have already visited.

Don't forget

The address bar displays the current location as a series of links, separated by arrows.

Hot tip

For common locations, you can type just the name, for example:
- Computer
- Contacts
- Control Panel
- Documents
- Picture

Create Folders and Files

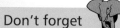

Don't forget

For this illustration, assume that Minutes were originally created and stored in the Documents folder, but needed to be stored in a folder of their own.

1 Open the drive or folder where the new folder is required, for example select Start, Documents

2 Click the Organize button and select the New Folder menu entry

3 Overtype the name New Folder with the required name and press Enter (or click elsewhere)

You can also create a folder or create a file from within the original folder.

Don't forget

The item you select will be created and named as New Folder or New Text Document, etc. Overtype this name as described above.

1 Right-click an empty part of the folder area and select New Folder or choose a particular file type

Copy or Move Files

You can copy a file using the Windows clipboard.

1. Open the folder containing the file, right-click the file icon and select Copy (to save the file path)

Hot tip

You could also select the file, and then click Organize, Copy. The keyboard shortcut for this is Ctrl+C.

2. Open the destination folder, right-click an empty space and select Paste to store the file

Hot tip

Alternatively, select the folder and then click Organize, Paste. The keyboard shortcut for this is Ctrl+V.

3. To move the file rather than make a copy, you'd right-click and choose Cut

4. The file icon will be dimmed until you select Paste, in the new location

Journal

Journal

Hot tip

The equivalent options are Organize, Cut and keystroke Ctrl+X.

...cont'd

To move or copy files using drag-and-drop operations:

1 Open the folder with the files you want to move

2 Select the first file then press the Ctrl key as you select the second and subsequent files

3 Click and hold any of the selected files, then drag the selection to the target folder and release there

4 To Copy rather than Move the files, hold down Ctrl as you drag and release the selection

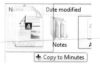

5 If the target folder is in a different drive, hold down Shift as you drag to Move, otherwise you will Copy

Delete Files

To remove files from a folder:

1 Select the file or files, right-click the selection and click Delete (or select Organize, Delete)

2 You'll be asked if you are sure

3 Click Yes to confirm

4 Files on the hard disk will be moved to the Recycle bin (files on other drives are removed immediately)

To recover a file deleted by mistake:

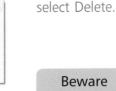

1 Right-click the Recycle bin and select Open, or simply double-click the icon

2 Select the file required and click "Restore this item"

3 Click "Empty the Recycle Bin" to remove files from the hard disk permanently and free up disk space

Hot tip

Pressing the keyboard Delete key will have the same effect as selecting the Delete menu entry.

Don't forget

To remove hard disk files completely without using the Recycle bin as an interim store, hold down Shift as you select Delete.

Beware

If the Recycle bin doesn't appear, see page 26 to show desktop icons.

Folder Views

1 Open the Documents folder, and note the file list style (in this case Details view)

2 Click the Views button and the file list changes (in this case to the Tiles view)

3 Click Views again and the list style changes again (to the Large Icon view)

The fourth style is a simple List view with small icons. Pressing the Views button will cycle through these four styles. To select a specific style:

1 Click the arrow next to the Views button and the full list is shown, with the additional Extra Large, Medium and Small Icons views

2 Select the required style, or drag the slider to obtain a custom size

The icons are based on the file type, except for image files, which use a miniature thumbnail of the actual contents, for example the Sample Pictures folder viewed as large icons.

Folder Layout

You can control which parts of the folder are displayed.

 Open the Documents folder in the usual layout, with the Navigation pane and Details pane displayed

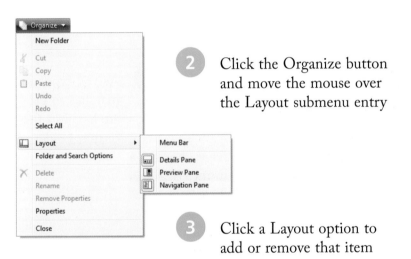

Click the Organize button and move the mouse over the Layout submenu entry

Click a Layout option to add or remove that item

For example, select Menu Bar and Preview Pane

Hot tip

To display the Contents pane only, as shown on page 92, click Details Pane and Navigation Pane to remove them.

Don't forget

This shows all the elements of a folder, including the Menu Bar familiar in previous releases of Windows.

Search Box

If you want to find a file, but are not sure which subfolder it is in, you can start at the higher-level folder and use the Search box to find the exact location.

1 Open the Music folder from the Start menu

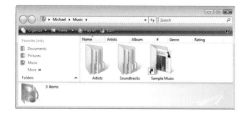

2 Click the Search box and start typing the search words, e.g. "Love is all around"

3 As you type, the matches so far are listed in the Search Folder

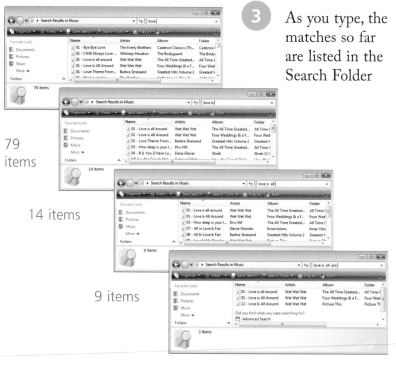

79 items

14 items

9 items

3 items

4 Stop typing when the results show the file you are seeking or when the window shows the whole list

Start Menu Search

If you don't have a starting point, or if the files you want are spread across several folders, then use Start Menu Search.

1 Click the Start button and type your search word(s), e.g. documents

2 Up to 20 results are listed (Programs, "Favorites and History", Files)

3 Click "See all results" to open the Search Folder and see more details and matches

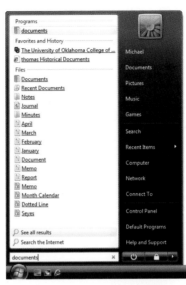

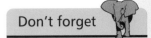

Don't forget

Start Menu Searches are applied to the Indexed locations on your system. These include your personal folders (Documents, Pictures, Music, etc.) and your email, but exclude program and system files.

Don't forget

If you press Enter, you'll open the top entry on the list of results, in this case the Documents folder.

4 The results are sorted by date modified, but you can click any of the file list headers to resequence the list

Hot tip

Click the header a second time, to sort the list in the reverse sequence.

Search Folder

Don't forget

You don't have to start with a search box in a folder or on the Start menu. You can go directly to the Search Folder.

To begin your search from within the Search Folder:

1 Select Start and click Search on the Start menu, to open the Search Folder

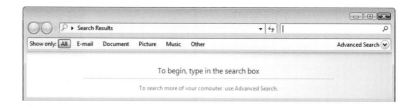

2 Type the search words into the search box

Hot tip

By default, the search will be in the Indexed Locations only, and all results will be displayed.

3 Click one of the filter buttons for example Music, to limit the list to particular types of file

...cont'd

With Advanced Search you can change the locations.

1 Click the Advanced Search button (which flips from the down arrow to the up arrow symbol)

Beware

With any location, you can click the box to include non-indexed and system files, but the search may take much longer.

2 Click the Location box and select to search the computer, a particular drive, or everywhere

3 Click Choose Search Locations to specify drives and folders

4 Click OK to apply the changes

Don't forget

You will find the Indexing Options in the Control Panel, under the "System and Maintenance" option.

Indexing Options
Change how Windows searches

To add a new indexed location:

1 Open Indexing Options, click the Modify button and select additional folders and subfolders for Windows to index

Folder and Search Options

The Organize menu also allows you to control the operation of folders and search tools.

1 From an open folder, click Organize and select "Folder and Search Options"

2 Select "Use Windows classic folders" to turn off Details and Preview panes (and add Menu Bar) for all folders

3 Select "Show preview and filters" to restore the panes

4 Select the View tab and click "Apply to Folders", to use the current folder settings for all your folders

5 Choose advanced settings such as "Always show icons, never thumbnails", or "Show hidden files and folders"

6 Clear the box "Hide extensions for known file types" to see file extensions as part of the file name

7 Click the Restore Defaults button to return to the original settings for your files and folders

7 Email and Calendar

Windows Mail provides the functions needed for secure and effective email communications. It also supports newsgroups (online forums). Windows Contacts provides the required address book functions. There's also Windows Calendar to keep note of tasks and meetings.

Electronic Mail

Email or electronic mail is used to send and receive text messages. You can send an email message to anyone with an email address, you can receive messages from anyone who knows your email address and you can reply to those messages, or forward them to another email address. You can send your email message to more than one person at the same time, and attach files such as documents or pictures.

Email is free, since no stamp or fee is required. However, before you can use email, you require:

- An account with an Internet Service Provider (ISP)
- An Internet connection such as telephone or cable
- A modem or router to make the connection
- An email address from your email service provider
- An email program such as Windows Mail

Windows Mail is the Windows Vista equivalent of the Outlook Express application found in previous releases of Windows. In addition to email, it also supports newsgroups. These are Internet-based discussion forums where members share information and opinions on topics of mutual interest. Windows Mail helps you read the messages posted by other members, and add your own messages to the forum for others to read.

To set up Windows Mail to use your email account you'll need the following information:

- Display name (appears at the top of email messages)
- Email address (created when you initially signed up)
- Server names (incoming and outgoing email servers)
- Server type (usually POP3 or IMAP)
- Password (also created when you signed up)

Don't forget

An email address consists of a user name or nickname, the @ sign, and the name of your email provider, such as jsmith99@myisp.com.

Hot tip

You can also send and receive email using your web browser, if the email account you use supports webmail (see page 113).

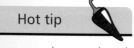

Don't forget

These details should be given to you by your email service provider. In some cases, the provider may update your Windows Mail settings automatically, so you don't have to enter the details.

Windows Mail

To add an email account to Windows Mail:

1. Click the Start button, then click the E-mail entry near the top of the Start menu

2. Windows Mail starts up and (if there's no email account already defined) it automatically prompts you for the details

Your Name

When you send e-mail, your name will appear in the From field of the outgoing message.
Type your name as you would like it to appear.

Display name: Vista for Seniors

For example: John Smith

Where can I find my e-mail account information?

[Next] [Cancel]

3. Type the name as you'd like it to appear in the From field in your email messages, then click Next

Internet E-mail Address

Your e-mail address is the address other people use to send e-mail messages to you.

E-mail address: vista4seniors@btinternet.com

For example: someone@microsoft.com

Where can I find my e-mail account information?

[Next] [Cancel]

4. Enter your full email address (the account name and the server address, separated by the @ symbol) then click Next to continue

Don't forget

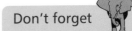

You need to be connected to the Internet (see page 116) to complete this operation. In this example there is an existing DSL connection.

Hot tip

If you leave this entry blank, your email address will be used for the From field.

Beware

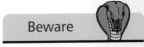

You must enter this address exactly as given, without spaces or changing capitalization.

...cont'd

The specifications for the email servers are dependent on the particular service, but the details shown are typical.

> Set up e-mail servers
>
> Incoming e-mail server type:
>
> POP3 ▾
>
> Incoming mail (POP3 or IMAP) server:
>
> mail.btinternet.com
>
> Outgoing e-mail server (SMTP) name:
>
> mail.btinternet.com
>
> ☑ Outgoing server requires authentication
>
> Where can I find my e-mail server information?
>
> Next   Cancel

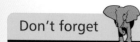

Don't forget

Click the box if you have been told that your outgoing server requires authentication.

5   Specify incoming server type (POP3 or IMAP) and name, and outgoing server name, then click Next

> Internet Mail Logon
>
> Type the account name and password your Internet service provider has given you.
>
> E-mail username: vista4seniors
>
> Password: ••••••••••••
>
> ☑ Remember password
>
> Next   Cancel

Beware

Some services require just the account name, while others ask for the full email address, so check the supplied details carefully.

6   Type the account name and password as specified by your email service provider, and click Next

> Congratulations
>
> You have successfully entered all of the information required to set up your account.
>
> To save these settings and download your e-mail, click Finish.
>
> ☐ Do not download my e-mail at this time
>
> Finish   Cancel

Layout

By default, Windows Mail opens with the Inbox selected, and there'll be at least one message, a welcome note from the Microsoft Windows Mail team.

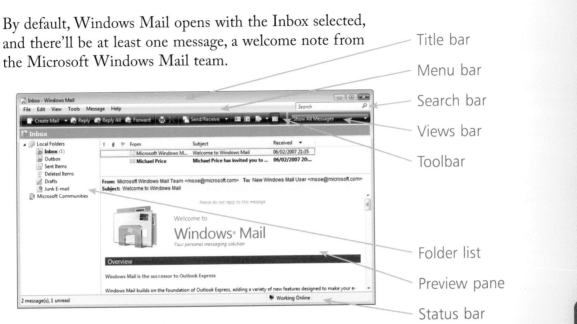

Title bar

Menu bar

Search bar

Views bar

Toolbar

Folder list

Preview pane

Status bar

The first entry in the message list is selected (highlighted) and the contents are displayed. If you'd prefer not to have messages automatically read, you can change the layout.

 Select View, Layout from the Menu bar

2 Clear the box labeled "Show preview pane"

3 Clear the boxes for other parts you may want to hide, and click Apply

Hot tip

Hiding the Preview pane reduces the chance of inadvertently opening messages that are spam.

Don't forget

The Folder Bar and the Views Bar will both be hidden if you have the default Windows Mail layout.

Receive Mail

You can check to see if there is any mail waiting for you on
the incoming mail server.

1 Start Windows Mail and click Send/Receive

2 Windows Mail connects to the Internet and initiates
retrieval of your email messages

3 The messages are added to your Inbox, latest first
(click the Received header to sort in reverse order)

View Message

1 Double-click an entry in the Inbox list to open the message (or select the entry and press Enter)

Hot tip

A highlighted entry is one that has not yet been read. The number in brackets after Inbox in the Folders list indicates how many such messages there are.

2 The message opens in a new window

3 To respond, click Reply on the toolbar

Don't forget

Click Reply to respond to the sender or click Reply All to respond to everyone who received the original message.

4 Type your reply and then click the Send button

Don't forget

The reply is moved to your Outbox and sent via your outgoing server the next time you Send/Receive. A copy is saved in your Sent folder.

Attachments

Some messages may have files attached, as indicated by the paperclip symbol alongside the Inbox entry.

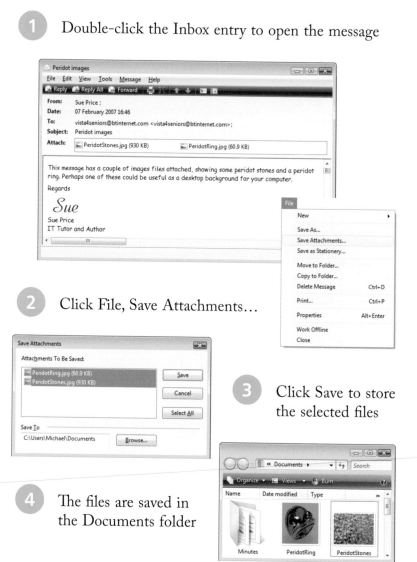

1 Double-click the Inbox entry to open the message

2 Click File, Save Attachments…

3 Click Save to store the selected files

4 The files are saved in the Documents folder

Windows Contacts

You can use Windows Contacts as the address book for
Windows Mail, to store and retrieve email addresses.

 Right-click any email address in a message, and
select "Add to Contacts"

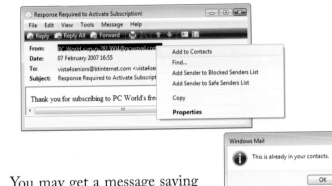

Don't forget

By default Windows
Mail will put people
you reply to into your
Contacts list.

2 You may get a message saying
this is already in your contacts

3 For new entries, the Contact Properties dialog opens,
with the email details already entered

Hot tip

You can click the
image, choose
"Change picture...",
and select a image
file, for example a
photograph. A
resized copy will
be stored with the
contact details.

4 No other details are needed for Windows Mail,
though you can add personal or employment related
information if needed. Then click OK to update the
Contacts list

Create a Message

1 Open Windows Mail and click Create Mail to open the new message composition window

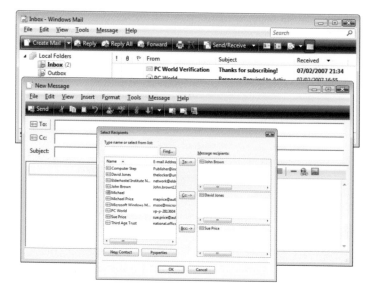

Hot tip

Recipients added using Bcc will not be shown on the copies of the message that others receive.

2 Click the To button to open the Contacts, then select names, pressing To, Cc or Bcc after each

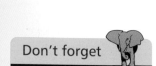

Don't forget

Select Tools, Options, Signatures to define the signature text to be automatically added to messages and replies.

3 Type the title for the message in the Subject box, type the message text and end with your signature

4 Press Send to finish (as with the reply on page 105)

Junk Mail Protection

Windows Mail will check your mail as it is received.

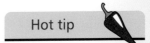

Hot tip

If you create a new message and close without sending it, the message will be saved in the Drafts folder.

1 Open the message with an attachment that has been saved as a self-extracting file, and Windows Mail removes access to it, just in case there's a virus

Beware

You'll still need an antivirus program to protect your system (see page 193).

2 Open Junk E-mail to check the messages transferred there and right-click to confirm the required action

Don't forget

Add the sender (or the sender's domain) to the blocked list or the safe list as appropriate, and return valid mail to the Inbox.

Newsgroups

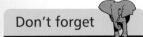

Don't forget

Microsoft Communities is the default news server in Windows Mail. Your ISP may provide a news server and there are others supported by special interest groups.

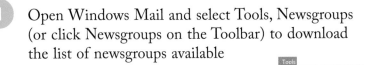

1 Open Windows Mail and select Tools, Newsgroups (or click Newsgroups on the Toolbar) to download the list of newsgroups available

Hot tip

Select the first entry then press and hold Ctrl while selecting further entries.

2 Specify a topic to list relevant newsgroups, choose those of interest and select Subscribe and then OK

3 Select the news server from the Folders list and click a newsgroup to review the message exchanges

Don't forget

You can simply read the messages, or you can add your own comments by selecting Reply Group.

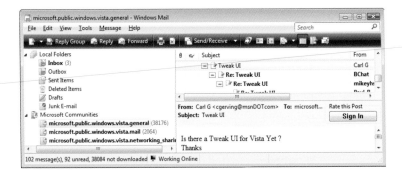

Windows Calendar

Windows Mail has a link to the Windows Calendar.

1 Select Tools, Windows Calendar or select the Calendar from the Toolbar

2 You can define appointments (including recurring appointments), create tasks and set reminders

3 There are no holidays or anniversaries defined, but you can download these in iCalendar format

4 For example, visit www.calendardata.com and select a calendar such as United States National Holidays

111

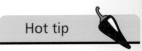

Hot tip

You can download holiday calendars for most countries, as well as specialized calendars such as sports fixtures.

Don't forget

Several formats are supported, but you should select the link for Windows Vista Calendar.

Subscribe to a Calendar

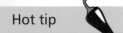

Hot tip

When you subscribe to a calendar at a website, Windows Calendar is started automatically.

1 Click Allow, to permit the website to open web content using Windows Calendar

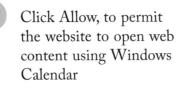

2 Confirm that the required calendar has been selected and then click Next

3 The required data is downloaded from the website to your system

4 Where appropriate, you can adjust settings such as update frequency, then click Finish

5 The requested calendar will be added to your Windows Calendar for the supported period, in this case three years

Don't forget

The events in the downloaded calendar will appear alongside the entries in your calendar.

6 Switch to month view to locate the added events

Webmail

You can access some email accounts using Internet Explorer rather than Windows Mail. This means that you can read and send email anywhere that you have Internet access. This could be an Internet cafe, at a hotel or using a wireless hot zone, at an airport for example.

Your ISP will provide details for accessing your account as webmail over the Internet, if this function is supported. Otherwise, you can provide yourself with an account just for webmail. Google for example offers free webmail accounts.

Don't forget

See Chapter 8 for more details of the Internet Explorer web browser

 Go to www.gmail.com and enter your username and password if you already have an account

 Otherwise, select "Sign up for Gmail" and provide requested details, including login name and password

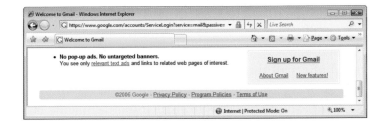

Hot tip

Google will suggest variations of the login name that are available, if your suggested name is already in use.

3 Click Check availability to validate your proposed login

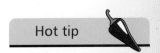
check availability!

...cont'd

When you've completed your registration and received your email you can sign in to the www.gmail.com website.

1 Double-click messages to open and read them

2 Select Compose Mail to create a new message

3 Click Contacts to select recipients or to add new email addresses

Webmail offers all the functions available in Windows Mail. As well as being accessible from anywhere on the Internet, it also allows you to check your mail and attachments before they are downloaded to your hard disk. However, it does require that you are connected to the Internet throughout the time that you are reviewing your mail.

8 Internet

The addition of tabbed browsing helps you navigate through the Web without losing track of useful web pages. The Favorites Center includes history as well as favorites. You can specify your preferred search engines and use the page zoom feature to focus on detailed contents.

Connect to the Internet

To set up an Internet account on your computer:

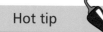
1 Click the Start button, select Control Panel, Network and Internet, then select "Connect to the Internet"

Network and Internet
View network status and tasks
Set up file sharing

Internet Options
Connect to the Internet | Change your homepage | Manage browser add-ons
Delete browsing history and cookies

2 The "Connect to the Internet" wizard starts up and asks the type of connection, e.g. Broadband or Dialup

Connect to the Internet

How do you want to connect?

Broadband (PPPoE)
Connect using DSL or cable that requires a user name and password.

Dial-up
Connect using a dial-up modem or ISDN.

Help me choose

Cancel

3 Select the type, provide details, e.g. phone number (dialup only), account name, password and click Connect to complete the connection definition

Connect to the Internet

Type the information from your Internet service provider (ISP)

Dial-up phone number: [Phone number your ISP gave you]   Dialing Rules

User name: [Name your ISP gave you]

Password: [Password your ISP gave you]

☐ Show characters
☐ Remember this password

Connection name: Dial-up Connection

☐ Allow other people to use this connection
This option allows anyone with access to this computer to use this connection.

I don't have an ISP

Connect   Cancel

Browse the Web

Windows Vista provides Internet Explorer v7.0 as the default Web browser.

1 Click the Start button then click Internet, at the top of the Start Menu

2 Internet Explorer opens and displays your Home page (the default startup website), in this example www.nga.gov

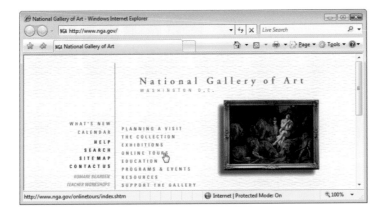

3 Move the mouse pointer over the window and where it changes to the hand symbol there's a hyperlink that you can click to view to another web page

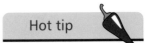

Hot tip

Alternatively, to start Internet Explorer click the icon on the Quick Launch bar, double-click the shortcut on the desktop, or select Internet Explorer from Start, All Programs.

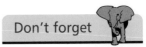

Don't forget

The Home page on your system is usually specified by your PC supplier or your ISP, but you can set your own (click the arrow next to the Home button).

Don't forget

You'll see the hyperlink address on the Status bar. Hyperlinks are often underlined and differently colored, to make them stand out.

117

Navigating

Hot tip

The Back and Forward buttons allow you to switch between pages.

Don't forget

Hyperlinks can be associated with images, and tool tips may be used to explain the purpose of the link.

Don't forget

Selecting Open Link will display the page in the same window, just as when you click a hyperlink. Pressing Ctrl when you click is the same as selecting Open Link in New Tab.

1 Click Back to return to the previous web page

2 Click and drag the scroll bar or click the scroll bar buttons to view other parts of the web page

3 Right-click the hyperlink and select "Open Link in New Tab" to display the specified web page in the same window but on a separate tab (see next page)

4 "Open Link in New Window" will display the page in a new Internet Explorer window

Tabbed Browsing

When you select "Show Link on New Tab", the new tab is added but the original tab remains displayed.

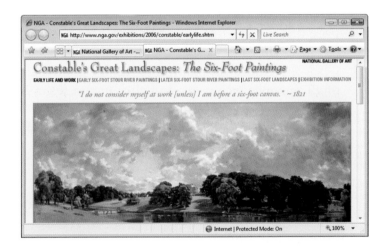

1 Select the new tab to view the web page it contains

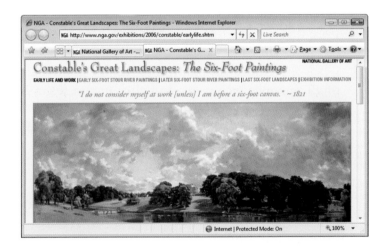

2 Select the first tab, then choose other hyperlinks and open them in new tabs, and click the New Tab button at the end of the tab bar to open a blank tab

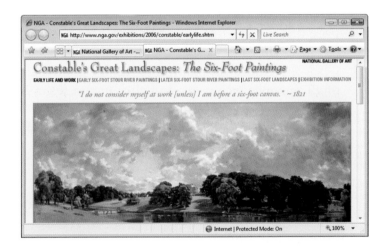

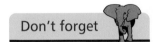
With Ctrl+Click, the tab opens in the background. If however you press Ctrl+Shift+Click, the new tab opens in the foreground.

Hot tip

If you have a mouse with a wheel, you can click a hyperlink with the wheel to open a new tab.

Quick Tabs

Hot tip

The Quick Tabs button is only displayed when you have more than one web page open. The Scroll buttons are only displayed after the Tabs row is filled.

When you have a number of tabs open, their titles become truncated and some tabs may be hidden. To help you select the tab you want, the Quick Tabs and Scroll buttons are added to the Tab row.

1 Click the Scroll buttons to cycle through the tabs

2 Click the arrow next to the Quick Tabs button to select a tab based on the web page title

NGA National Gallery of Art -- Online Tours
NGA American Impressionism: Introduction - NGA
NGA NGA - Cézanne in Provence: Introduction
NGA The Dance Lesson by Edgar Degas
NGA Rembrandt's Late Religious Portraits
NGA NGA - Constable's Great Landscapes: The Six-Foot Paintings
✓ **Welcome to Tabbed Browsing**

3 Click the Quick Tabs button to display thumbnails of all the open web pages and click one to select it

Don't forget

The thumbnail image sizes are automatically adjusted to fit the width of the Internet Explorer window (three across usually).

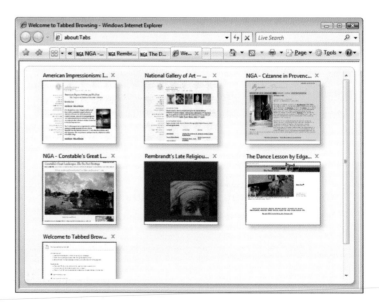

4 Click the Quick Tabs button to close the thumbnails view and redisplay the last web page viewed

Close Tabs

1 To close the current tab, click the X on the tab (or press Ctrl+W or press Alt+F4)

Hot tip

From the Quick Tabs view, click the X on any thumbnail to close that web page.

If you have a wheel mouse, click a tab on the tab row with the wheel to close that tab.

2 To close all the tabs except the current tab, press Ctrl+Alt+F4

3 To close the Internet Explorer session, click the X on the window title bar, or click the icon on the left and select Close or press Alt+F4

	Restore	
	Move	
	Size	
—	Minimize	
▫	Maximize	
x	**Close**	Alt+F4

4 If there's more than one tab open, you will be prompted to confirm that you want to close all tabs

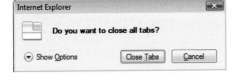

Internet Explorer

Do you want to close all tabs?

⊙ Show Options   Close Tabs   Cancel

Don't forget

Click the Cancel button if you decide you do not want to close all the tabs at this time.

5 Click the Show Options button

Internet Explorer

Do you want to close all tabs?

☐ Open these the next time I use Internet Explorer
☐ Do not show me this dialog again

⊙ Hide Options   Close Tabs   Cancel

6 You can choose to open the same set of web pages, the next time you start Internet Explorer

This is useful for continuing work in progress, but if you will need the same set of web pages again, save them as a group.

Add to Favorites

When you visit a web page that you'll want to view again in future, you can save it as a Favorite.

1 With the web page displayed, click Favorites and select the "Add to Favorites…" menu entry

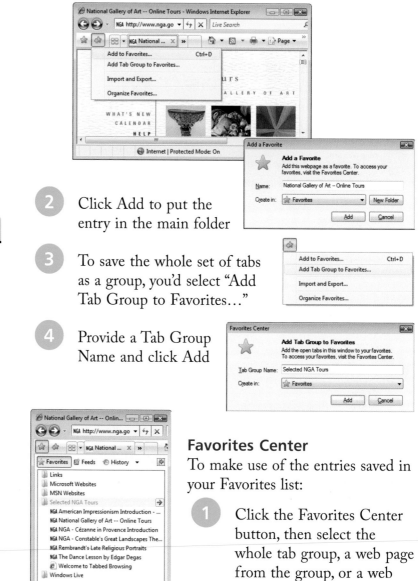

Hot tip

You can select a different Favorites folder from the list or create a new folder.

2 Click Add to put the entry in the main folder

3 To save the whole set of tabs as a group, you'd select "Add Tab Group to Favorites…"

4 Provide a Tab Group Name and click Add

Favorites Center

To make use of the entries saved in your Favorites list:

1 Click the Favorites Center button, then select the whole tab group, a web page from the group, or a web page saved individually

Search for Websites

You can type website addresses on the address bar but the easiest way to locate a website is to use the Search bar.

1 Type key words into the search box, for example "Saks 5th Avenue", and press Enter

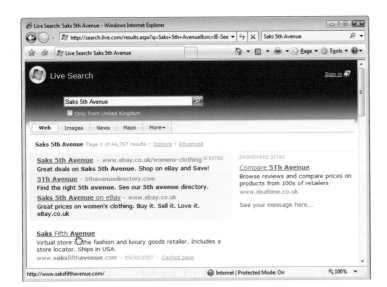

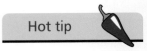

Beware

The first few results are sponsored sites and paid adverts, so look below these for the websites that best match the search text.

123

2 Click the link in the header to go to the website

Hot tip

If the header that you select doesn't show the web page that you want, press the Back button (or click the initial tab) and choose another entry from the search results.

3 Follow hyperlinks in the web page to open other pages on the same tab or in new tabs (see page 119)

Alternative Search Providers

By default, Internet Explorer uses Microsoft's Live Search but you can choose a different search provider.

1 Click the arrow next to the Search box and select Find More Providers…

2 Click a provider, for example Yahoo.com, and click the Add Provider button.

3 Click a provider such as Google, click the box Make this my default provider, and click Add Provider

4 The default provider will be updated

5 To use one of your alternatives, click the Search box arrow and select the provider, which will stay as the active provider for the remainder of the session, unless you make another change

Page Zoom

You may find some web pages difficult to read, especially if you have your monitor set for high resolution. The Page Zoom feature provides an effective solution to this problem.

1 Click the arrow next to Zoom on the status bar

2 Choose the zoom level, for example 200%

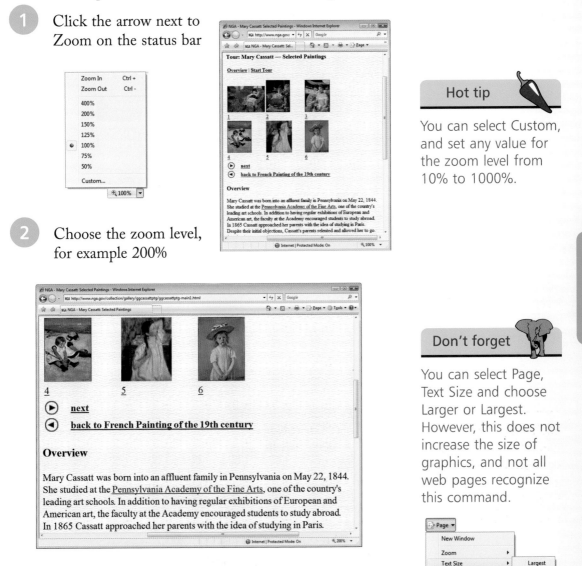

Hot tip

You can select Custom, and set any value for the zoom level from 10% to 1000%.

Don't forget

You can select Page, Text Size and choose Larger or Largest. However, this does not increase the size of graphics, and not all web pages recognize this command.

3 Click Zoom to revert to the 100% zoom level

4 Note that clicking the Zoom button repeatedly will cycle through levels 125%, 150% and 100%

Print Web Page

1 Open Internet Explorer, navigate to the web page and make sure that it is displayed on the active tab

Don't forget

Internet Explorer will automatically adjust the print size to fit the width of the paper, so that none of the contents will be truncated. In this example, a factor of 83% is required.

2 Click the arrow next to the Print button and select the Print Preview... option

If Shrink To Fit makes the web page too small to read comfortably, you can change the page orientation and the scale factor, for example:

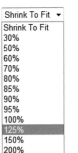

1 Select the Landscape button in Print Preview... then click the Shrink To Fit box and select a scale factor such as 125%

Hot tip

Select Custom, and set any value for the scale factor between 30% and 999%.

Hot tip

To see the Shrink To Fit value, select Shrink To Fit then select Custom, and the setting will be shown.

127

2 To see more pages at once, click the Page View box and select the appropriate number of pages, e.g. 6

3 To print part of the web page, highlight the area, click the arrow next to the Print button and choose Print...

4 For the Page Range pick Selection then click the Print button

Hot tip

To print a picture from the web page, right-click the picture and select Print Picture... Then click the Print button.

RSS Feeds

An RSS feed (also known as a web feed) is a means of collating updates to web pages so you can be made aware of changes without having to revisit the website. Internet Explorer tells you whenever there's a feed available.

 If there are no feeds available, the Feeds button on the toolbar will be grayed

2 When you switch to a web page that has a feed, the Feeds button changes color and a sound plays

CNN - Top Stories [RSS] (new)
CNN - Recent Stories [RSS] (new)

3 Click Feeds to view the reports and to subscribe

4 Change the name for the feed if desired, then click Subscribe

5 Your subscription will be confirmed

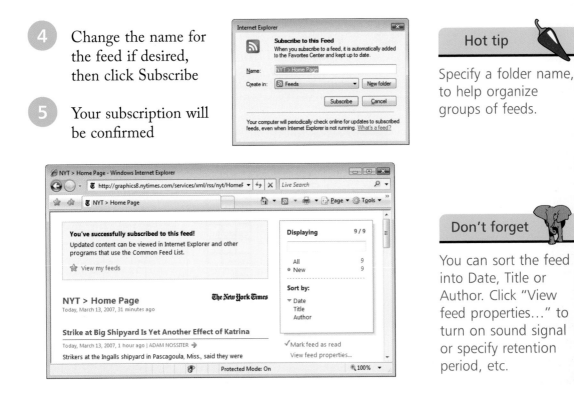

129

6 To view your subscribed feeds, click the Favorites Center button and then click Feeds

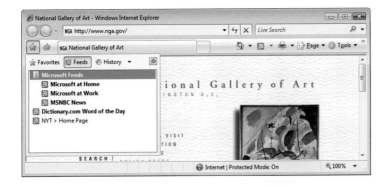

7 Subscriptions with new content are highlighted

8 Click any entry to review its contents

Hot tip

Specify a folder name, to help organize groups of feeds.

Don't forget

You can sort the feed into Date, Title or Author. Click "View feed properties..." to turn on sound signal or specify retention period, etc.

Beware

Your computer will periodically check for updates, even when Internet Explorer is not running.

History

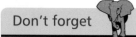

1 Click the Favorites Center button, select History and click the green arrow to pin the Favorites Center

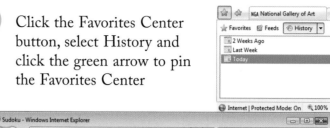

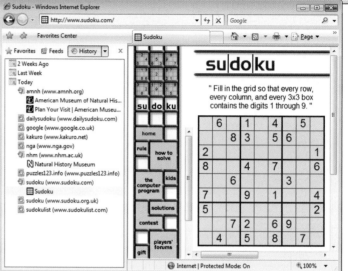

2 Click a period, e.g. Today, click a website header to list the web pages visited, then select a web page

3 To clear the history, click the Tools button, select Delete Browsing History... and click the Delete buttons

9 Windows Applications

Windows includes some surprisingly useful applications for calculating, text editing, word processing and picture editing, but you need external programs to handle files unknown to the default setup.

Applications

Windows provides the operating environment for a variety of applications. In many cases, these are supplied as separate programs or suite of programs. However some of the desired functions may be included with Windows, in the form of small but potentially very useful programs. The main application areas, and the related Windows programs are:

- Text processing   NotePad
- Word processing   WordPad
- Electronic Mail   [see chapter 7]
- Drawing   Paint
- Spreadsheet   Calculator only
- Database   [no program]
- Multimedia   [see chapter 12]

For requirements not supported by the programs in Windows, you'll need to install separate programs or a suite of programs. We look at readers and viewers, free programs that allow you to view files from other applications such as Adobe Acrobat and Microsoft Word.

Calculator

While no substitute for a spreadsheet application, the Windows Calculator does provide computational facilities.

1 Select Start, All Programs, Accessories, Calendar

2 Type or click to enter the first number, the operation symbol and the next number

3 Enter any additional operators and numbers and press = to finish

You click the calculator buttons or press the equivalent keyboard keys, to perform Add, Subtract, Multiply, Divide, Square Root, Percent and Inverse operations. You can also store and recall numbers from memory.

There is a Scientific version of the calculator:

1 Open Calculator, select View, Scientific and choose the number system, e.g. Dec and Degrees

The Scientific calculator allows conversions between number systems, performs functions such as logarithms and factorials and includes statistical calculations

2 Select View, Standard to return to the normal mode

Don't forget

You can also use the numeric keypad to type numbers and operators. Press Num Lock if it is not already turned on.

Don't forget

The scientific calculator supports hexadecimal, decimal, octal and binary numbers.

Hot tip

Calculator clears the display when you switch between standard and scientific. Use the memory button to transfer a number between the two modes.

NotePad

Notepad is a text editor that you can use to create, view or modify text (.txt) files. It provides only very basic formatting, and handles text a line at a time.

Hot tip

The absence of formatting turns into a benefit when you are working with the source files for a program or the HTML code for a web page, since these require pure text.

1 Select Start, All Programs, Accessories, NotePad and type some text, pressing Enter to start a new line

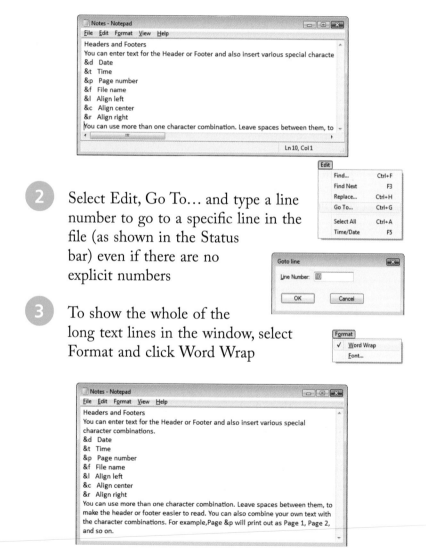

2 Select Edit, Go To… and type a line number to go to a specific line in the file (as shown in the Status bar) even if there are no explicit numbers

3 To show the whole of the long text lines in the window, select Format and click Word Wrap

Beware

The Go To… function is grayed and disabled, and the Status bar is hidden, when you select the Word Wrap option.

4 When you print the file, it will wrap according to the paper width, regardless of the word-wrap setting

WordPad

WordPad also offers text-editing, but adds tools and facilities for complex formatting of individual pieces of text.

1 Select Start, All Programs, Accessories, WordPad and enter text, pressing Enter to start a new paragraph

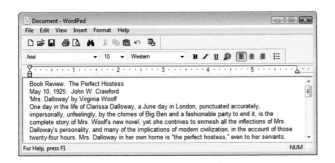

Hot tip

You can copy text from other documents or from a web page, using standard Copy and Paste operations.

2 Use the formatting bar to change the font, size, style and color for selected (highlighted) text

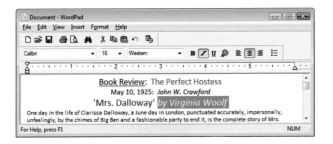

Hot tip

Click the left, center or right alignment button to adjust the positioning of the selected paragraph or line of text.

3 Click the Save button (or select File, Save, or press Ctrl+S) to write the file to the disk

4 You must save WordPad documents as .rtf (Rich Text Format) to retain the text formatting

Don't forget

WordPad documents can be saved as .txt (text) but text formatting (and any images or links) with be stripped out.

...cont'd

WordPad also allows you to include pictures in documents.

1 Position the typing cursor where you want the picture and select Insert, Object...

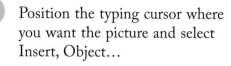

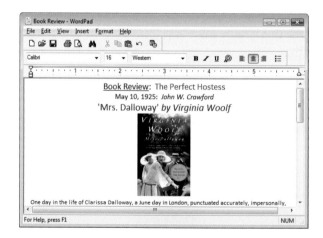

2 Select Create from File, locate the picture file and select the object type (e.g. Paintbrush Picture) and click the Link box (but leave Display As Icon clear)

A copy of the picture is added to the text. It is linked to the original file so that any changes to that file in the future will be reflected in the WordPad document.

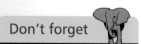

JPEG Image

3 If you select the Display As Icon box, a shortcut will be inserted, and you can click this to display the picture

mrs_dalloway

Paint

Paint is a digital sketchpad that can be used to draw, color and edit pictures. These can be images that you create from scratch, or you can modify existing pictures, such as digital photographs or a web page graphics. For example:

Hot tip

 Select Start, All Programs, Accessories, Paint to open a blank canvas and click Image, Attributes

Although it is a simple image editor, Paint can be used to create very complex images, a pixel at a time if required.

2 Set the canvas size (e.g. 800 by 500 pixels) and click OK

3 Select Edit, Paste From, locate a picture that will fit on the canvas and click Open

cutty-sark
JPEG Image
13.6 KB

Don't forget

If the pasted image is larger than the canvas, the canvas will automatically be extended to hold the picture.

4 Drag the image to the upper middle of the canvas

...cont'd

5 Select the Rounded Rectangle tool then click and drag to draw a frame around the picture

6 Use the Text tool to draw a text box and add information such as a description of the contents

7 To edit fine details in your pictures, select Zoom, Custom and choose a suitable scale factor

8 Or use the Magnifier tool

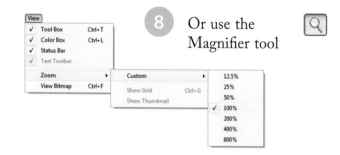

9 When you've finished making changes, select File Save, type the file name and click Save

Unknown File Types

The Windows applications may be useful for some tasks, but they cannot help when you download files or receive attachments of unknown file types. For example:

 If there are unknown file types in your Documents folder, the extension (normally hidden) is displayed

Don't forget

Windows supports a set of file types (as indicated by the file extension). If you have additional programs installed, there may be further known file extensions on your system.

139

 Double-click an unknown file type and you get a warning that Windows cannot open this file

Hot tip

When the application search is unable to find the type, it will suggest the website www.filext.com, which has a more comprehensive list.

Click OK to use the Web service to display details of the file type and suggested programs to open it (see page 140 for .pdf information and page 142 for .doc)

Portable Document Format

The application search provides information for .pdf files.

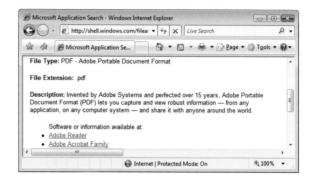

1 To view the contents of .pdf documents, select Adobe Reader and click Download Adobe Reader

2 Choose Save to download the file and write it onto your hard disk

3 Double-click the downloaded file to install Adobe Reader

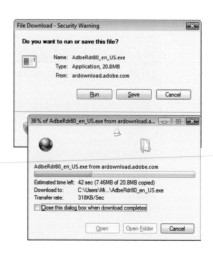

AdbeRdr80_en_US

4 Follow the prompts to install and configure the Adobe Reader application

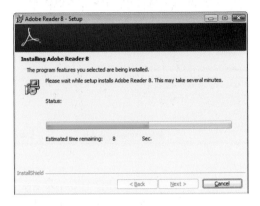

5 Click Finish to exit Setup and launch Adobe Reader

Don't forget

An entry for Adobe Reader will be added to the Start menu under All Programs. There will also be a shortcut icon added to the desktop.

6 You will now be able to open and read .pdf files

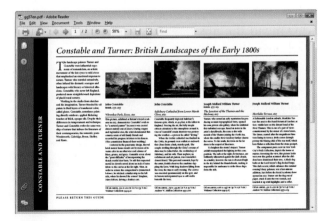

Word Document Files

Application search also provides suggestions for .doc files.

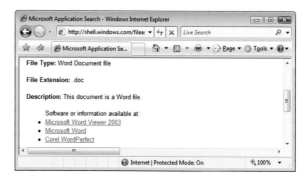

1 To view the contents of .doc documents, select Word Viewer 2003 (which also handles Word 2007 files)

2 Download the installation file and save it on your hard disk

...cont'd

3 Double-click the downloaded file to install Word Viewer

4 Follow the Setup program prompts to complete the installation and configuration of Word Viewer 2003

Don't forget

An entry for Microsoft Office Word Viewer 2003 will be added to the Start menu under All Programs.

5 You will now be able to open and read .doc files

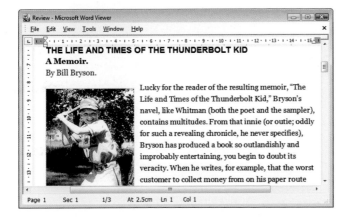

Note that files that were shown with file extensions will now have their extensions hidden, once they become known.

Beware

Word Viewer will also become the default program for .rtf (Rich Text Format) files previously handled by WordPad.

Microsoft Office 2007

Microsoft Office 2007 was launched at the same time as Windows Vista. As with Vista, Office 2007 is provided in a number of editions, culminating in the Ultimate edition, which has the fullest set of application programs.

When Office 2007 is installed under Windows Vista, a new folder called Microsoft Office is added to the Start menu, with entries for all the application programs. There is also a subfolder called Microsoft Office Tools.

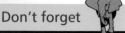
Don't forget

Other editions include:
- Basic
- Home & Student
- Standard
- Small Business
- Professional
- Professional Plus
- Enterprise

These contain subsets of the applications that are in Ultimate.

144

Hot tip

Like Vista, Office 2007 has removed the Menu bar in the main applications. However, the changes go further and affect the toolbar structure.

The most notable new feature of Office 2007 is the "Microsoft Office Fluent graphical user interface" (also known as Ribbon), which replaces the conventional menus and toolbars. This result-oriented user interface is incorporated in the core applications: Word, Excel, PowerPoint, Access and some parts of Outlook. Other applications will be upgraded to the new user interface in subsequent versions.

To view the new user interface:

1. Click Start, All Programs, Microsoft Office and select one of the upgraded applications, for example Microsoft Office Word 2007

2 The application window participates in the Windows Aero scheme if activated on your system

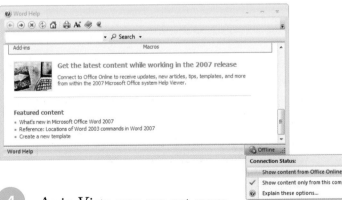

Quick Access toolbar

Title bar

Command tabs

Help button

Office Ribbon with commands

Groups

Mini toolbar (semi-transparent)

Layout buttons

Zoom slider

Status bar

Word count

3 Click the Help button or press F1 to show the Help window with a list of general topics, and use the Search box to get answers to more specific queries

Don't forget

The Office button replaces the File command and supports common tasks such as Open, Save, Print and Share.

4 As in Vista, you can get more up-to-date help information from the Internet

Change Default Program

You may wish to change the default program associated with a particular file type. For example, you may wish to restore WordPad as the default for .rtf files.

 1 Right-click any .rtf file and select Open With

2 Choose the program to use, check the box "Always use the selected program to open this kind of file" and click OK

Hot tip

To open a file with a particular program, without changing the default, clear the box then click OK.

3 The files now have WordPad as the default

Don't forget

Files of type .doc will still have Word Viewer as the default, as indicated by the program icon.

10 Windows Games

*Windows provides
an endless source of
entertainment, for you or
the grandchildren. There's
a wide variety of games to
both challenge and teach.*

Games Explorer

The Games Explorer identifies the games supplied with Vista or installed on your computer and provides access to them via the Games Folder.

Hot tip

Third party games that are compatible with Windows Vista will register themselves during installation so that they can appear in the Games folder.

Don't forget

Premium games (Chess Titans, Inkball, Mahjong Titans and Purble Place) are in Vista Home Premium and Ultimate editions. Hold 'Em is one of the Ultimate Extras (see page 196).

148

1   Click the Start button and select Games to display the Games folder with all the games on your system

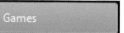
Games

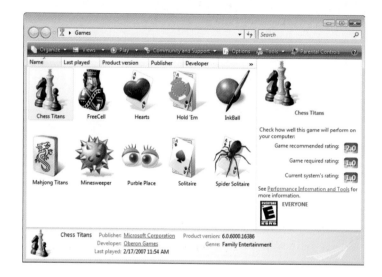

2   The Details pane shows information such as the publisher, developer and version

3   The Preview pane shows hardware needs and the game ratings

4   The games supplied with Vista are all rated as Everyone (3+) except for the optional Hold 'Em poker game, which is rated as Teen (12+) because it includes simulated gambling

Don't forget

The games use the ESRB (Entertainment Software Rating Board) ratings or the local equivalent, for example PEGI (Pan European Game Information) in Europe.

 PEGI 12+

 PEGI 3+

Chess Titans

1 Double-click Chess Titans in the Games folder to begin a game (or continue the last game)

Hot tip

You can play against the computer or against another person (who would share your mouse to make moves).

2 Click a piece to see the legal moves (these are colored blue, or red where you can take a piece)

3 Click Game to choose a new opponent, change appearance or resign a game

Game
New game against computer F2
New game against human F3
Undo Ctrl+Z
Statistics F4
Options F5
Change Appearance F7
Resign
Exit

4 Click Options to change graphics quality and other settings

Don't forget

Chess Titans keeps track of all the games you play and shows your results when you select statistics.

Options

- ● Play against computer as white
- ○ Play against computer as black

Difficulty

Level 1 — Level 10

- ☑ Display animations
- ☑ Play sounds
- ☑ Show tips
- ☐ Always continue saved game
- ☐ Always save game on exit
- ☑ Show last move
- ☑ Show valid moves
- ☑ Rotate board when playing head to head
- ☐ Top down view
- ☑ Rotate board back after free view

Graphics quality

- ☑ Show 3D view
- ☑ High detail pieces
- ☑ Show reflections
- ☑ High gloss shine
- ☑ Smooth edges

OK   Cancel

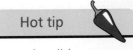

Hot tip

Drag the slider to the left to turn off graphics quality options progressively.

Mahjong Titans

It is simpler to get started with this game and it needs only one player. However, it takes a surprising amount of strategy and planning to achieve high scores.

1 Double-click Mahjong Titans in the Games folder

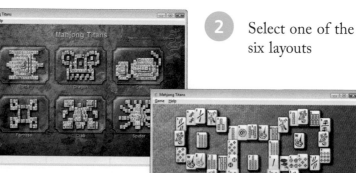

2 Select one of the six layouts

3 Click matching pairs of free tiles to remove them

4 If you (or your grandchild) get stuck, select Game, Hint and two matching tiles will flash

New Game	F2
Undo	Ctrl+Z
Hint	H
Statistics	F4
Options	F5
Change Appearance	F7
Exit	

5 Select Change Appearance to choose an alternative background and tile set

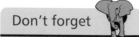

Traditional Tiles   Primary Color Tiles   Pastel Tiles   Large Print Tiles

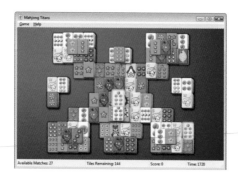

6 Fireworks are displayed when you complete a game

Minesweeper

1 Double-click Minesweeper in the Games folder

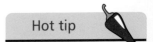
Click a square on the playing field. If a number appears on a square, it indicates how many total mines are in the eight squares that surround the numbered square.

2 If you uncover a mine, you've lost the game

Don't forget

You use the number to help deduce whether a square is safe to uncover. Right-click a suspect square to add a flag, or double right-click to a ? mark.

151

3 Click Play again for a new game, or Restart this game to try it again

Don't forget

Choose flowers as an alternative to mines, but they'll still explode if you click on them.

4 Click Game to start a new game, view the statistics, adjust the options or change the appearance

Purble Place and InkBall

Purble Place

This is educational and entertaining, helping to teach colors,
shapes, and pattern recognition. Players can choose beginner,
intermediate or advanced, and to play against the clock.

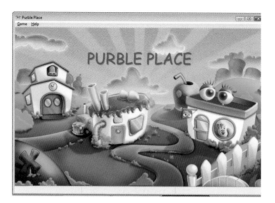

 Double-click Purble Place, and select one of the
games (Purble Pairs, Comfy Cakes and Purble Shop)

InkBall

The goal is to get bouncing balls into holes of the same
color. The player steers the balls by deflecting them with ink
strokes that are drawn with the mouse (or tablet pen). If a
ball goes into the wrong hole, the game is over!

1 Double-click InkBall
and select the difficulty
level (Beginner,
Novice, Intermediate,
Advanced and Expert)

2 Points are awarded
based on the colors
of the balls (from red
200 up to gold 1600)

FreeCell

FreeCell is a variant of solitaire. To win, you must stack the four suits in ascending order (ace to king). You draw cards from seven columns of cards that you build in descending order, alternating red and black. Free cells are used to hold cards temporarily while you rearrange sequences.

 Double-click FreeCell to deal out a random game (or continue with a previously saved game)

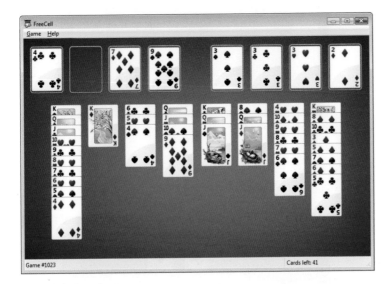

2. Click Game, Select Game and enter a game number between 1 and 1,000,000

3. Click Game, Change Appearance to select a new card deck or background

Windows includes four card games, all of which are designed for a single player.

No solutions have yet been found for games: 11,982, 49,192, 186,216, 455,889, 495,505, 512,118, 517,776 or 781,948. All other games are solvable.

Each of the four card games has a Change Appearance command that offers the same choice of card decks and backgrounds.

Other Card Games

Hearts

You play in rounds against three computer opponents. The aim is to avoid taking the hearts and the queen of spades.

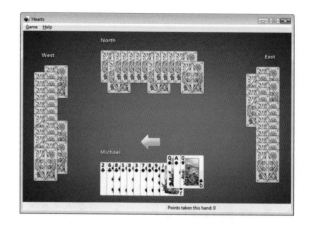

Solitaire

Solitaire is based on the traditional Klondike solitaire.

Spider Solitaire

Spider Solitaire uses two decks (104 cards).

11 Music and Audio

Create recordings, play audio CDs and convert tracks to computer files. Build and manage a music and sound library.

Sound Card and Speakers

Hot tip

You can also open System Properties by selecting "View computer details" in Welcome Center.

The sound card in your computer processes the information from programs such as Windows Media Player and sends audio signals to your computer's speakers. To identify your card:

1. Press Windows Logo+Pause keys to open System Properties, and click Device Manager

2. Click the [+] next to "Sound, video and game controllers" to see the sound card that is installed

Don't forget

You may have sound features incorporated into the main system board, rather than on a separate adapter.

3. To configure your sound setup, open Control Panel and select "Hardware and Sound", and then Sound

 Hardware and Sound
Play CDs or other media automatically
Printer
Mouse

Sound
Adjust system volume
Change system sounds
Manage audio devices

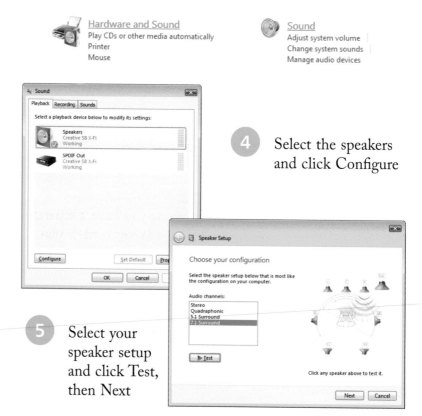

4. Select the speakers and click Configure

5. Select your speaker setup and click Test, then Next

6 Specify which speakers are present in your setup

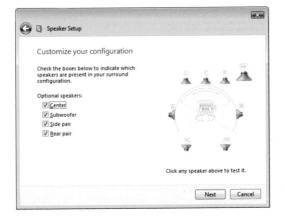

Hot tip

When you specify a stereo (two speaker) setup, you can select satellite or full-range speakers.

7 Click Finish to complete the configuration

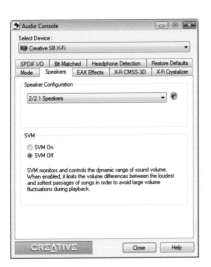

8 If you have a separate adapter card, it may be supplied with an audio application program to help you configure and test the audio setup

Don't forget

For a Creative sound card, select Start, All Programs and look for the Creative folder in the Start menu.

Recording

With a sound card on your system, you can make voice recordings from a microphone or other audio sources. To set up your microphone:

 Open the Sound option from the Control Panel (see page 79) and click the Recording tab

Select the Microphone entry and click Configure

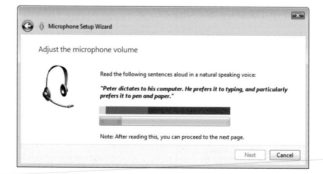

Select "Set up microphone" to run the wizard

Choose the type of microphone (headset, desktop or other), read the sample text and follow the prompts to set up the microphone for best recordings

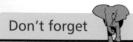

Don't forget

Other sources could include Line-In (audio device), Digital-In (CD or DVD drive) or What U Hear (anything that is being played through the sound card, including web broadcasts for example).

Don't forget

Select Start, Speech Recognition to run the wizard that sets up voice control on your computer.

Don't forget

A headset microphone is the best choice if you are considering use of voice control.

If the microphone recording level is too low:

1 Click the Microphone Properties button on the Sound Recording panel

[Properties]

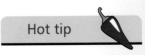
Hot tip

The Properties button is on the Recording tab for the Sound dialog (see page 158).

2 Click the Custom tab and select the 20dB Boost

Microphone Properties

General | Custom | Levels | Advanced

Microphone

Change Icon...

Controller Information

XFi Creative SB X-Fi   [Properties]
Creative Technology, Ltd.

Jack Information

No Jack Information Available

Microphone Properties

General | Custom | Levels | Advanced

☑ Microphone +20dB Boost

[OK] [Cancel] [Apply]

Device usage: Use this device (enable)

[OK] [Cancel] [Apply]

Make a Recording

1 Click the Start button, search for Recorder and select Sound Recorder

Programs
🎵 **Sound Recorder**

Sound Recorder
● Start Recording   00:00:00   ❓ ▾

Hot tip

Alternatively select Start, All Programs, Accessories and then click Sound Recorder.

2 Click Start Recording button and say your message

Sound Recorder
■ Stop Recording   00:00:54   ❓ ▾

3 Click Stop Recording and provide a name for the audio file that will be created

Save As
◀ Users ▸ Michael ▸ Documents ▸   Search
File name: Verbal note
Save as type: Window Media Audio File
Artists: Personal   Album: Comments on report
▸ Browse Folders   [Save] [Cancel]

159

Don't forget

The file is created as type Windows Media Audio (.wma). Specify the originator as the Artist and put a description as the Album.

Windows Media Player

Hot tip

Click the Start button and select All Programs, and you will find Windows Media Player towards the top of the Start menu.

Don't forget

Leave the boxes clear if you'd prefer not to send information about your playing experiences.

To play the recorded sound file:

1. Open the folder containing the file, and double-click the file icon to start Windows Media Player

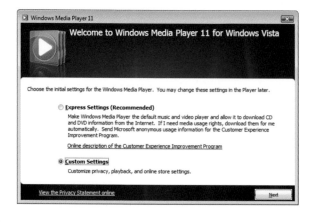

2. The first time, you must choose Express Settings (for default values) or Custom Settings (to set your own)

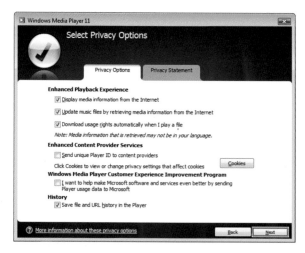

3. Make any changes you wish, then click Next

4. You can choose to add a shortcut to the desktop or the Quick Launch bar, and to make Windows Media Player the default music and video player

...cont'd

The recorded item plays in Windows Media Player. It is treated as if it is a music track, and it quotes any artist and album details that you provided when you created the file.

 Click the arrow below Now Playing to show options

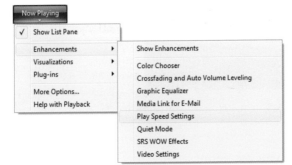

Don't forget

Selecting any of these will turn on the Show Enhancements option. Click the arrows to scroll through the enhancements.

2 Click Enhancements, Play Speed Settings

3 Move the Play Speed slider, or click the Slow, Normal or Fast link to select the playback speed

Hot tip

You can speed up a voice recording to get an overview or slow it down to help with note taking. The sound maintains correct pitch when the playback speed changes.

Play Audio CD

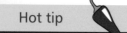

Hot tip

If you leave the box checked to "Always do this for audio CDs", Windows Media Player will be used automatically the next time you insert this type of disc.

1. Insert an audio CD and close the drive

2. Windows recognizes the type of disc and asks you what to do (if the default action hasn't already been defined)

3. Choose "Play audio CD using Windows Media Player" and the program starts up, playing the CD

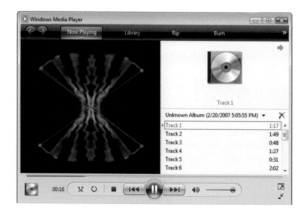

Don't forget

The next time you play this CD, Windows Media Player will recognize it and display the details without having to access the Internet.

4. If you are connected to the Internet, the player will identify the specific disc and download track details

Copy Tracks

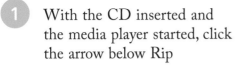

1 With the CD inserted and the media player started, click the arrow below Rip

Rip 'Discovery' (E:)

Format ▸
Bit Rate ▸

Rip CD Automatically When Inserted ▸
Eject CD After Ripping

More Options...
Help with Ripping

2 Select Format and choose the type of audio file (for example MP3)

Windows Media Audio
Windows Media Audio Pro
Windows Media Audio (Variable Bit Rate)
Windows Media Audio Lossless
✓ MP3
WAV (Lossless)

3 Select Bit Rate and choose the desired quality (e.g. 192 Kbps)

128 Kbps (Smallest Size)
✓ 192 Kbps
256 Kbps
320 Kbps (Best Quality)

4 Click Rip then click Start Rip

5 Each track in turn is copied, converted and saved

163

Music Library

The converted tracks will be saved in the Artist/Album subfolder of the specified location, e.g. the Music folder.

Don't forget

In this illustration, the artist Mike Oldfield has two albums, Discovery and Ommadawn.

To play the tracks from the hard disk:

1. Select Start, All Programs, Windows Media Player and click the Library button

2. Choose how to display the contents of the music library, for example by Album or Artist

Hot tip

Right-click an album and select Play or "Add to Now Playing".

12 Pictures and Videos

Import digital images (photos or videos) from your camera or from media memory cards. Windows Photo Gallery helps you organize your collections. For the most complete media system, use Windows Media Center.

Digital Pictures

There are a number of ways you can obtain digital pictures:

- Internet (e.g. art and photography websites)
- Scanner (copies of documents, photographs or slides)
- Digital Camera (photographs and movies)
- Email attachments and faxes

Website pictures will usually be stored as JPEG (.jpg) files, which are compressed to minimize the file size. This preserves the full color range but there is some loss of quality. Some images such as graphic symbols and buttons will use the GIF (.gif) format, which restricts color to 256 shades to minimize the file size.

To copy a digital image from a website:

1 Right-click the image and select Save Picture As...

2 Type a suitable file name and click Save

Don't forget

Using TIFF (.tif) format will retain the quality level, but the files will be larger. However, Internet Explorer does not support the TIFF image format.

Hot tip

You can right-click and save the picture even when only part of it is visible on the screen.

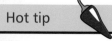

Hot tip

Click Browse Folders to select a folder and create a subfolder, e.g. using artist name, to organize the saved images.

3 Select Start, Pictures and select the appropriate subfolder to view the saved images

Hot tip

You can also view your downloaded pictures in the Windows Photo Gallery (see page 170).

4 Some websites prohibit you from saving their image files to disk

Beware

Images downloaded from websites are usually copyrighted and provided for personal use only.

5 Other websites go out of their way to make it easy, even providing a choice of image sizes, in this case ranging from 160 x 107 (6 KB) to 1680 x 1120 (944 KB)

Don't forget

The galleries at the www.pbase.com and www.psa-photo.org websites give insight into the range of possibilities for digital photography.

167

Beware

If your camera isn't recognized by Windows you must install the software that was supplied with the camera. This may provide its own way of copying pictures.

Don't forget

The date of transfer will be used as the folder name, and the pictures are renamed as 001, 002, 003, etc. The tag is appended to these names, helping to provide a unique file name.

Import from Camera

To transfer pictures from your camera to your computer:

1 Connect the camera to a USB port on your computer, and turn on the camera

2 The required device driver is installed

> Installing device driver software
> Click here for status.
> Installing device driver software
> EN   14:32

> Your devices are ready to use
> Device driver software installed successfully.
> ...ice driver software
> EN   14:33

3 Select the option to "Import pictures using Windows"

AutoPlay

Removable Disk (K:)

☐ Always do this for pictures:

Pictures options

Import pictures
using Windows

View pictures
using Windows

View pictures
using Windows Media Center

General options

Open folder to view files
using Windows Explorer

Set AutoPlay defaults in Control Panel

4 Specify a tag word to apply to all the pictures (you can add more tags after the transfer)

Importing Pictures and Videos

Tag these pictures (optional):
BVI

Options   Import

Importing Pictures and Videos

Removable Disk (K:)

Importing item 20 of 29
☐ Erase after importing

Cancel

5 The pictures are copied to disk

Michael ▸ Pictures ▸ 2007-02-23 BVI   Search

Organize ▾ Views ▾ Slide Show Burn

Favorite Links   Name   Date taken Tags   Size   Rating
Documents
Pictures
Music
More »

Folders   BVI 001   BVI 002   BVI 003   BVI 004   BVI 005   BVI 006

29 items

Media Card Readers

If your camera uses a removable memory card such as
Secure Digital or Compact Flash, you may be able to read
the card directly, without having to attach the camera.

 Attach a media card reader to your computer (or use
the media card reader built into the computer)

Hot tip

Using a card reader
instead of attaching
the camera directly will
avoid running down
your camera battery.

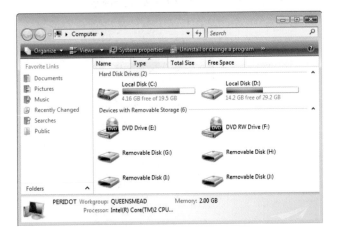

The Dell E520 computer for example has a media card
reader installed in the place of a floppy drive. The reader can
handle a variety of types of memory card. There are four
slots to handle the different sizes and each slot has a drive
letter associated with it.

2 Insert the memory card into the reader and the
AutoPlay dialog is displayed (as with the camera)

3 Select "Import pictures using Windows" to copy
picture files from the media card drive to Pictures

Don't forget

Whichever method
you use, when the files
are copied, Windows
Photo Gallery opens
with Recently Imported
selected (see page 170
for details).

169

Windows Photo Gallery

Hot tip

Windows Photo Gallery displays pictures and videos, mainly from the Pictures folder. Initially, it shows pictures that are recently imported.

To change the displayed selection:

1 Click the triangle next to a category heading such as Tags or Date Taken to expand the list of values

Don't forget

Tags are descriptive words associated with particular pictures. You can have several tags associated with each picture, giving a variety of ways of selecting pictures.

2 Choose, for example, the Wildlife tag to see all associated pictures and videos

Hot tip

Move the mouse over a particular file to see an enlarged thumbnail with details including the file name, the size and the list of tags.

Add Tags

1 Display the pictures you want to tag (e.g. by date taken or by folder) and select one or more images

Don't forget

You can specify tags when you import pictures. In that case, the tags are also appended to folder and file names.

Hot tip

You can also click the Info button and then click the Add Tags button.

2 Right-click the selection and choose Add Tags, then type a tag word, or select a previously used tag

Don't forget

The Info pane shows the tags associated with the selected pictures. Note that the new tags have been added to the Tags list.

Fix Pictures

1 Double-click any picture to enlarge it

2 Click left and right arrows to scroll through the pictures, and click Fix button to make adjustments

3 Click Auto Adjust, or select the individual tools to make changes, and press Back To Gallery to save, or Undo to cancel the amendments

Burn to Disc

If you have a CD or DVD writer on your computer, you can make copies of your pictures, as data files or as a slide show.

1 Select the pictures that you want to save then click the Burn button and choose the type of copy

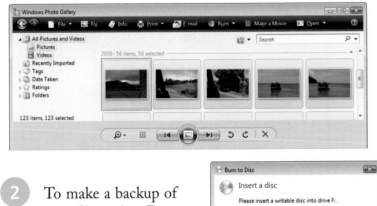

2 To make a backup of your files, select Data Disc… and insert a CD or DVD when prompted

3 Click to "Show formatting options", and select Mastered

4 Click "Burn to disc" to complete the transfer

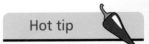

Hot tip

Use Ctrl to select multiple files (see page 90). If there are duplicate file names such as 001.jpg, Windows may amend names during copy to 001.jpg(2), etc.

Don't forget

Using the Mastered format creates a CD or DVD that can be read by previous versions of Windows and by other devices such as CD and DVD players.

Hot tip

The picture files will be written to the root folder of the CD. Folder structure isn't maintained.

Video DVD

To create a slide show, perhaps with music or commentary:

1 Display the pictures in Windows Photo Gallery

2 Click the Views button, select Sort By and choose a suitable sort order, such as Date Taken

3 Select the pictures required and click Burn, Video DVD...

4 The selected pictures are added to a new Windows DVD Maker project

5 Provide a disc title (the default is the creation date)

6 Click "Add items", and select additional pictures, or choose music or speech files to accompany the show

7 Click Next to change styles and to Preview the show

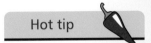

8 Click Burn and insert a blank DVD, and the slide show will be created

9 Click the Close button when the DVD is completed

Windows Movie Maker

To create more advanced movies on your computer:

1 Click Start, All Programs, Windows Movie Maker

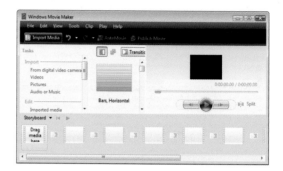

2 Click Import Media to select video clips or pictures

3 Add transitions, effects and audio tracks

| AutoMovie | |
Name	Description
Fade and Reveal	Applies fade and reveal transitions
Flip and Slide	Applies flip, slide, reveal, and page ...
Highlights Movie	Cuts, fades, adds a title and credits
Music Video	Quick edits for fast beats and long....
Old Movie	Film age effect applied to clips
Sports Highlights	Selects action clips and adds a title...

Windows Media Center

Windows Media Center is an integrated entertainment complex that provides support for digital media of all types. With it you can listen to music or radio, watch TV, play a CD or DVD or manage your picture and video collections.

 1 Click Start, All Programs, Windows Media Center to start (Setup may run the first time you do this)

welcome

To get started with Windows Media Center, select one of the following setup options:

- Express setup
- Custom setup
- Run setup later

set up tv

2 The categories of media function are listed, including Pictures+Videos, Music, TV+Movies, Online Media

Pictures + Videos

Music

more music · music library · play all · radio

TV + Movies

3 Select Pictures+Videos to work with your photos or video clips, sorting by folder or by tag

picture library

▶ play slide show
‹ folders › tags date taken

2007-01-27 R · 2007-02-26 V · Documents
2007-02-23 B · 2007-03-15 A · ample Pictur
2007-02-25 St · Constable · Various

Pictures : 2007-03-15 Amalfi
3/15/2007 69 items

177

...cont'd

4 Select Music for the music library (and radio tuner)

5 This is where you'd use your TV tuner if installed, but it is also used for playing DVD movies

6 Online media includes Internet TV, movies, music, radio news, sports and games

13 Networking

Create a home network, wired or wireless, to share folders, printers and Internet connections. Windows Vista ensures that the network you set up is safe and effective. You can even include your old XP computer.

Create Home Network

You have a network when you have several devices that exchange information over a wire or over radio waves. The simplest network consists of one computer and a router that links to the Internet. You can add a second computer, to share the Internet access and to exchange information with the other computer. If you have an older computer running a previous version of Windows, you can add it to the network.

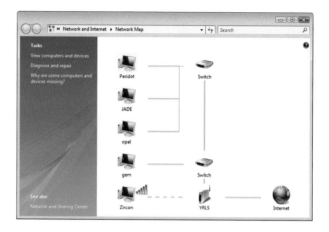

To make the connections your network will require:

1. Ethernet twisted-pair cables, for the wired portion

2. A router to manage the network connections

3. An Internet modem, which may be integrated with the router

4. An adapter for each computer (wired or wireless)

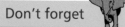
To implement your network, you'll need to carry out actions such as these:

- Install the necessary network adapters
- Establish the Internet Connection
- Set up the wireless router
- Connect the computers and start Windows

Wired Connection

1 Install the network adapter (if required) and start up Windows (with no network connection)

2 The icon on the system tray shows the adapter is currently disconnected

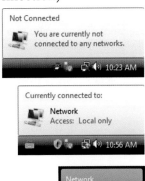

3 Add a cable between the adapter and the router

4 Click the Start button then select Network

5 If network discovery and file sharing is turned off, click the message and then select to turn them on

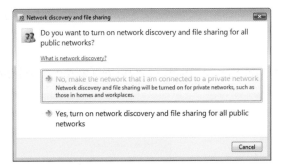

6 Choose to turn on network discovery and file sharing for private networks (e.g. home or office)

Don't forget

Often, there will be a network adapter built into your computer. Otherwise, you'll need to install an adapter card or add a USB network adapter.

Beware

Don't turn on file sharing for a network detected in a public place such as a coffee shop or airport.

Change Network Settings

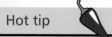
1   Click the "Network and Sharing Center" button

2   Click Customize to change the network name

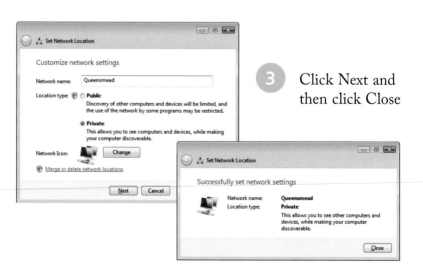

3   Click Next and then click Close

Set up the Router

The network is renamed as specified. You can now use the computer to set up your router for Internet and wireless

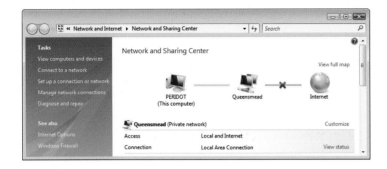

1 Open Internet Explorer and enter the address for your router, for example http://192.168.1.1

2 Type the administration user name and password and click OK

3 This will start the program to set up the router

4 Follow the prompts to configure the router for Internet or wireless operation as needed

Hot tip

Some routers also offer USB connection so that you can configure them before the network is set up.

Don't forget

This is an IP (Internet protocol) address that is hard-coded in the hardware. Your hardware supplier will provide this address.

183

Don't forget

Your router may be provided with a configuration program, or you may be able to access the router via the network connection.

Wireless Connection

Hot tip

Normally you need to install the necessary device driver software before you install or attach the wireless adapter.

If your router includes wireless capability, you'll need to set up wireless adapters for the appropriate computers.

 Insert the configuration CD for your wireless adapter

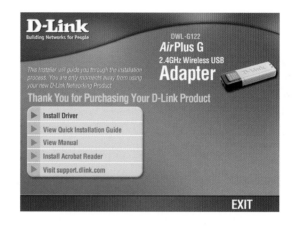

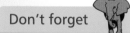

Don't forget

The details will depend on the specific device that you are installing but this illustrates the typical process.

Select Install Driver and follow the prompts

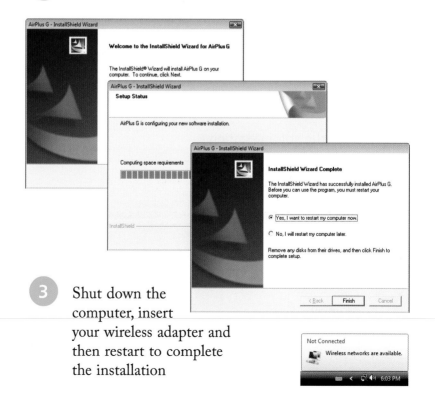

Shut down the computer, insert your wireless adapter and then restart to complete the installation

Connect to the Network

1 Right-click the network icon in the system tray and select "Connect to a network"

2 Select the desired network and click Connect

3 Type the phrase or password for the network and click Connect

4 Click Close to save the network

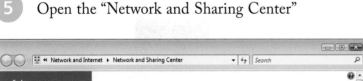
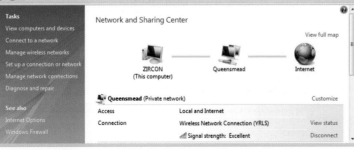

5 Open the "Network and Sharing Center"

Hot tip

You could click Start, Network and select "Network and Sharing Center" then click the link "Connect to a network".

Beware

Your system may detect other wireless networks that are in the vicinity, so make sure to select the correct entry.

185

Don't forget

Select Customize from the "Network and Sharing Center" to change the network name or to make the network Private. Note also that the Internet connection will be enabled if you have configured the router.

Network Map

1 Click Start and select Network then select the "Network and Sharing Center"

Don't forget

This shows the two connections (wired and wireless) that have been defined.

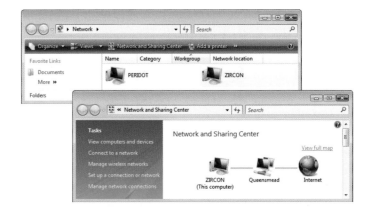

2 Click the link "View full map" to see the connections

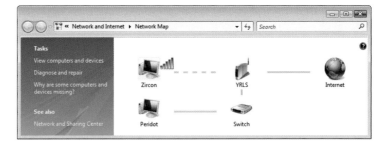

Hot tip

This may not show all connections, if for example "Password protected sharing" is switched on (the default setting).

3 In "Network and Sharing Center", expand "Password protected sharing", click Turn Off and click Apply

...cont'd

4 When "Password protected sharing" is turned off, you may see additional computers on your network

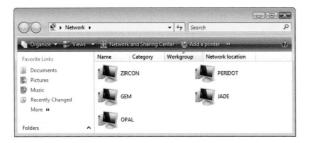

5 Some computers may not be correctly placed on the map, for example those running Windows XP

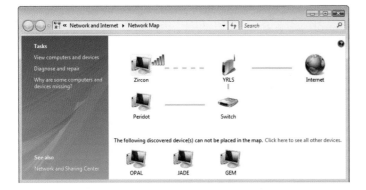

6 Visit www.microsoft.com/downloads and search for LLTD Responder and download the installation file

Hot tip

Right-click the window and select Refresh to show recently powered-on computers.

Don't forget

Network Map in Windows Vista uses the Link Layer Topology Discovery (LLTD) to query other devices on the network. This update will install the LLTD Responder component on Windows XP-based computers.

187

Windows XP Computers

1 Install the LLTD update on each of your Windows XP computers in turn (no need to restart the computers)

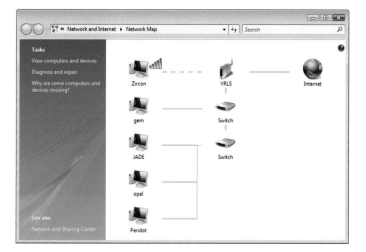

2 Open the "Network and Sharing Center" and redisplay the network map to see the changes

Don't forget

This maps the network from the wireless connection. The map on page 180 shows the same network from the wired connection.

Hot tip

Windows Network Diagnostics help you identify and resolve issues that may arise with your network, such as connection problems.

3 If there are still problems, select "Diagnose and repair"

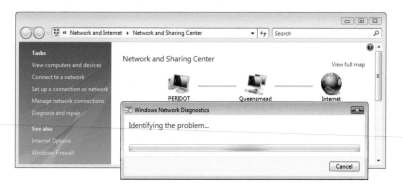

Share Folders

To make a folder or a drive available for sharing:

 1 Locate and select the folder or drive you want to share, right-click the selection and choose Share

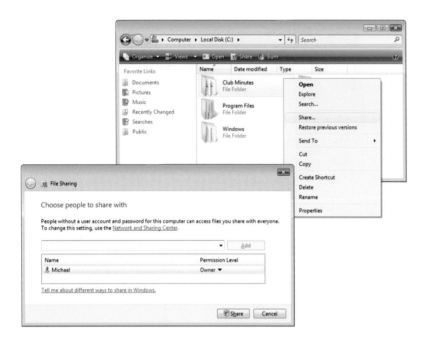

2 If you have "Password protected sharing" switched off, any users on your network can access shared items

3 If required, select the Email link to notify selected users that you have resources available for sharing

Don't forget

From the "Network and Sharing Center", you can turn on sharing for files and folders, public folders, printers and media files.

Sharing and Discovery		
Network discovery	On	
File sharing	On	
Public folder sharing	On	
Printer sharing	On	
Password protected sharing	Off	
Media sharing	On	

Hot tip

In a similar manner, right-click a device in the Printers folder and choose Sharing.

Xerox DocuPrint-M750
0
Ready

Beware

If "Password protected sharing" is switched on, only selected users with accounts on the computer can use the shared items.

Access Shared Folders

1 From a networked computer, select Start, Network and double-click the computer with shared devices

2 If password protection is switched on, you'll need to enter your user name and password and click OK

3 The items available for sharing will be listed

The Public folder is the place in Windows where you store files that you want to share with other users on the same computer or with users on the network.

14 Security & Maintenance

Windows Security Center helps protect your system from hazards on the Internet. Backup and restore tools protect against disk failures.

Windows Security Center

There are a number of security features in Vista, and these are monitored in the Windows Security Center. You'll be alerted by an icon in the notification area.

1 Double-click the icon to open the Security Center to view the current status and adjust settings

2 Windows provides a Firewall to help protect your system from other computers on the Internet

3 "Automatic updating" ensures that your copy of Windows has all the critical updates (see page 195)

4 "Malware protection" guards against problems caused by malicious software such as spyware and viruses

5 Other security settings monitored include "Internet security settings" and User Account Control

...cont'd

If there's no antivirus software installed:

1 Click the "Find a program" button in the Security Center

2 Click one of the suppliers listed for details of Vista-compatible programs, usually with free trials

3 Alternatively, visit free.grisoft.com to download AVG, which is free for private, home computer use

4 When you've installed antivirus software, the "Malware protection" warning will be removed

Don't forget

Click the Worldwide link to list antivirus software suppliers for other locations.

Worldwide

Hot tip

Download the setup program to your hard disk and run it from there, following the prompts to install and configure AVG.

Windows Firewall

Hot tip

You can go straight to the Exceptions tab if you select Start, Control Panel and click "Allow a program through Windows Firewall", in Security.

Security
Check for updates
Check this computer's security status
Allow a program through
Windows Firewall

Beware

If you have additional security software that includes its own firewall, make sure only one is running at any given time.

Don't forget

Programs may be added automatically when applications are installed, for example the AVG programs for providing daily updates.

1 Click the Windows Firewall link in Security Center to view the current settings

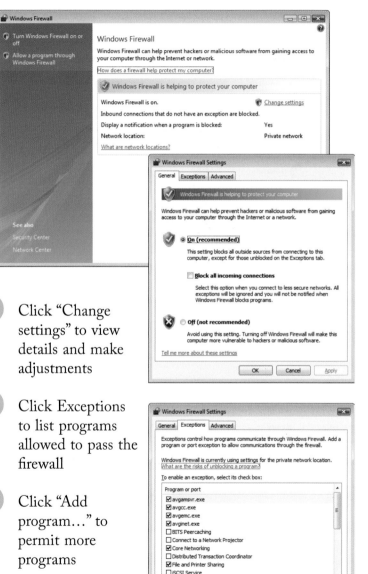

2 Click "Change settings" to view details and make adjustments

3 Click Exceptions to list programs allowed to pass the firewall

4 Click "Add program…" to permit more programs

5 Click OK to save changes and exit

Windows Update

To check for updates to Windows:

1 Click the Windows Update link in Security Center

Hot tip

Updates are changes or additions that will help fix or prevent problems, enhance operation or improve performance. They can be large, e.g Service Pack 1 (SP1) issued in March 2008 was in excess of 65 MB.

2 Click "Check for updates", and you can download and apply the updates that are available

Beware

If Windows Update is not switched on, you'll see an alert in the Notification area.

3 Select Change Settings to select "Install updates automatically"

Don't forget

If you have a DSL connection, choose the Automatic option. Otherwise, select the "Check for updates" option.

Windows Ultimate Extras

If you have the Ultimate edition of Windows Vista, you can download some special programs. To see what's available:

Hot tip

Ultimate Extras are downloaded via Windows Update but must be requested individually.

1 Check for updates using Windows Update

Don't forget

The Extras available at any time will vary. You may also find updated versions of existing Extras that you've previously downloaded.

2 Click View available extras

3 Select the extras you want and click Install

4 The programs are downloaded and installed

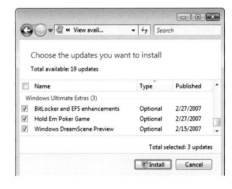

Hot tip

Windows DreamScene allows video clips for desktop backgrounds, but only if your system is capable of running Windows Aero.

5 Restart the system if required to complete the installation of the programs

Microsoft Update

When you install Microsoft Office 2007 (see page 144) it recommends that you sign up for Microsoft Update.

Hot tip

If you do not want to sign up at the time of installation, click the box labeled "I don't want to use Microsoft Update".

This extends Windows Update (see page 195) to include automatic updates for Office and other products that are installed on your computer. To activate Microsoft Update, if not selected during the Office installation:

1 Select Start, All Programs, Windows Update (or select "Check for updates" in Control Panel)

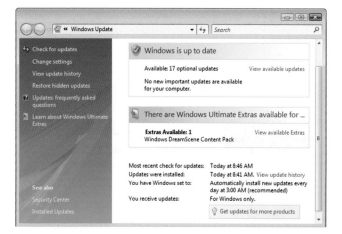

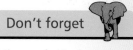

Don't forget

Microsoft Update supports updates for:
- Windows
- Microsoft Office
- MSN
- Windows Server
- SQL Server
- Exchange Server
- Visual Studio

2 Scroll down to the bottom and click "Get updates for more products", which is shown when Microsoft Update isn't yet activated

...cont'd

3 Click the box to accept the terms and conditions and then click the Install button

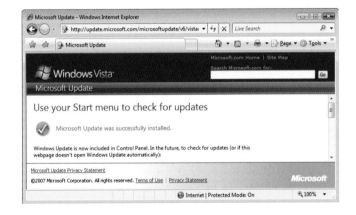

4 Microsoft Update will be installed and enabled

5 Microsoft Update checks for and installs updates for Windows and other Microsoft products

System Restore

Problems may arise when you install new software or a new device. If uninstalling does not correct the situation, you can return the system files to their values prior to the changes.

1 Click Start, All Programs, Accessories, System Tools and select System Restore, or click Start, type "system restore" and press Enter

2 System Restore will offer to reverse the most recent change (normally the best course of action)

3 If the problem originated at an earlier time, click "Choose a different restore point" and click Next

Hot tip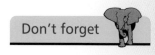

Restore points are created every day and just before any significant change such as an installation or update. You can also open System Protect and create a restore point yourself.

199

Don't forget

Select a date and time that's prior to the problems and click Next to apply the change.

Backup and Restore

You can lose files accidentally, as a result of a virus, or due to software or hardware failure. To protect your files, you should make backup copies.

Don't forget

You'll need a suitable backup device, such as a CD or DVD writer, or a second hard disk, preferably external so it can be kept in a separate location.

1 Click Start, All Programs, Maintenance, Backup and Restore Center

2 Create backup copies of particular types of files, or take a complete backup of your whole system

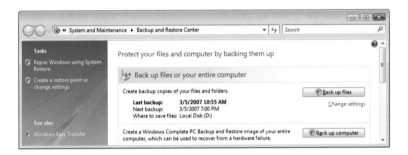

Hot tip

Click Start, All Programs, Accessories, System Tools and select Backup Status and Configuration, to check the status of scheduled backups.

3 You can restore individual files or the entire system

Hot tip

Shadow copies of changed files are also created by System Restore when a restore point is created.

4 When you accidentally modify a file, right-click the file icon and select "Restore previous versions", to see what backup copies are available

15 Help & Support

Help and support is enhanced by online access to the latest information. There are also other ways of getting useful advice.

Windows Help

Most functions in Windows are supported by wizards, which make the tasks easier by providing prompts and suggestions. However, there is a comprehensive help system when you do need answers to questions.

1 Click the Start button and select "Help and Support"

2 Select one of the topics, open the table of contents, or type a query in the Search box

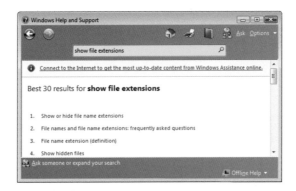

3 If you are currently using offline help (which is based on the contents of the Windows installation disc), you'll be recommended to connect to the Internet to get the most up-to-date information

4 Click the first of the top 30 entries (this is likely to be the most relevant)

5 Click the Offline Help button and select "Get online Help" (or click the "Connect to the Internet" message as shown on page 202)

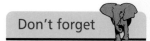

6 The button now indicates Online Help, and the list of results is updated with new and changed entries

Not all entries are equally relevant. There's an entry for Microsoft PowerPoint for example, which links to the presence of the word Show in the search text.

Guided Help

Hot tip

Guided Help is an interactive way to assist you to carry out a task. It is only available in Online Help.

Hot tip

You are recommended to select the step-by-step method as an effective way of learning the technique.

Don't forget

In this example, the Guided Help pauses for you to select whether you want to show or to hide file extensions.

1 Select the top result from the Online Help list, for an example of guided help

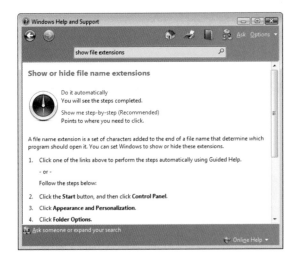

2 The computer can complete the task automatically, or direct you step by step through the procedure

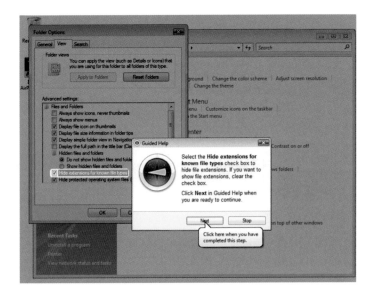

Even if you select the automatic method, it stops at appropriate points for you to make required selections.

In Context

You won't always have to search for the relevant help topics. Sometimes, the specific help you require is presented to you.

1 Select Start, Computer and then click the Help icon button on the toolbar

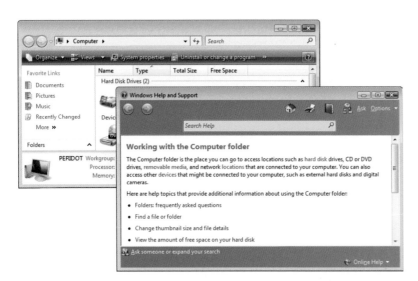

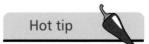
Hot tip

When you are carrying out a specific operation, the Help system will effectively carry out a search and automatically display the most relevant item.

2 Relevant help information is immediately displayed

3 There's a similar effect when you open a program such as WordPad and select Help from the menu bar

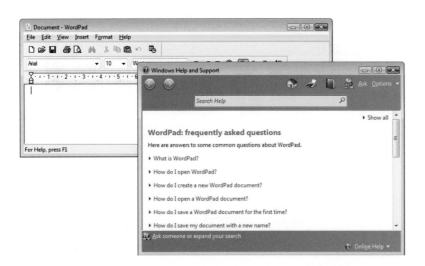

Don't forget

Pressing F1 while you are viewing a folder or a program window has the same effect as clicking the appropriate Help icon.

Ask a Friend

If you can't find the answer you are seeking in the Help information, ask someone else for help.

1 Open "Windows Help and Support", or click the Home icon if Help is already displayed

2 Scroll down to the Ask Someone section

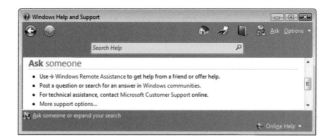

3 Use Windows Remote Assistance to invite someone to access your system and help solve your problem

4 Post questions to the Windows communities

5 Contact Microsoft Customer Support online

More Support Options

6 Click "More support options…" to get other resources

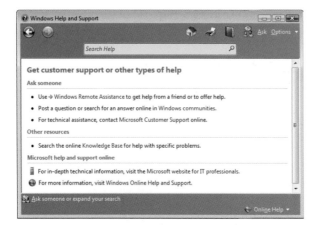

Hot tip

Search the Knowledge Base for help with a particular issue.

7 Click "Windows Online Help and Support"

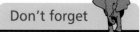

Don't forget

Click any of these topics for helpful advice and guidance.

8 Select Browse by edition, and choose your edition of Vista to review edition-specific information

Tips & Tricks

1 For more help and advice visit the Vista website
www.microsoft.com/windows/using/windowsvista

2 Click the link "Get tips and tricks for Windows Vista"

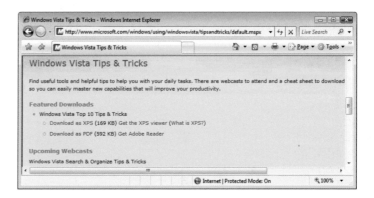

3 Download the Top 10 Tips & Tricks document

Index

G

H

I

Index

213

Y

Z